M4M

FOR AN HOUR OR FOREVER
THE GAY MAN'S GUIDE TO FINDING LOVE ONLINE

WITHDRAWN

JACK MAURO

SIMON SPOTLIGHT ENTERTAINMENT
NEW YORK   LONDON   TORONTO   SYDNEY

S|S|E

SIMON SPOTLIGHT ENTERTAINMENT

An imprint of Simon & Schuster

1230 Avenue of the Americas, New York, New York 10020

Copyright © 2004, 2007 by Jack Mauro

SIMON SPOTLIGHT ENTERTAINMENT and related logo are
trademarks of Simon & Schuster, Inc.

Book design by Yaffa Jaskoll

Manufactured in the United States of America

First Edition 10 9 8 7 6 5 4 3 2 1

Library of Congress Cataloging-in-Publication Data

Mauro, Jack.

M4M : for an hour or forever; the gay man's guide to finding love online / Jack Mauro.

p. cm.

ISBN-13: 978-1-4169-4072-2

ISBN-10: 1-4169-4072-3

1. Gay men—Computer network resources. 2. Gay online chat groups.

3. Dating (Social customs)—Computer network resources. 4. Internet—Social aspects.

I. Title. II. Title: M four M. III. Title: Em four em.

HQ75.14.M38 2007

646.7'70285469308664—dc22

2006024483

Deep gratitude is owed to Lilly Ghahremani, my agent, who saw a light when nobody else was even seeing a tunnel; to Patrick Price, my editor, who seems to own a blue pencil with some serious magic in it; to Adam, for scolding me when he saw a "Jack thing" happening; and to Maggie, beloved pooch, for having abandoned her habit of eating fast food discards off the sidewalks.

CONTENTS

M4M

PROLOGUE

Hallelujah! It's raining men! Every specimen!
— "It's Raining Men," The Weather Girls

I HAVE AN OLD FRIEND WHO LIVES IN MONTANA. GREAT state, Montana: beautiful, open, studded with glorious mountains, all of it. But not exactly swarming with gay cowboys, despite what outdoorsy porn films—or an Ang Lee film triumph—would have you believe. My friend has been alone, and for quite a while, and he is rather sick of it.

Just last week he asked me what he should do to meet guys. I wasn't all that sanguine about how I could help. But I had noticed that the membership of a certain gay dating website had grown a lot over the past year. True, only six months before, it had boasted not a single ad from men seeking men in my friend's neck of the woods. Yet . . . I suggested he have a look. He did. There were hundreds of ads from Montanans. The pioneers had made it to the West, and virtually overnight. I'm not sure he actually yelled it, but I think my old friend let out a hearty "Yippee!"

Fifteen years ago the options for meeting up with like-minded men were confined to a few bars, a tacky disco in a

1

bad part of town, and a notorious public bathroom in the mall. Ten years ago a few websites and a motley assortment of chat rooms opened the doors to a vast and very dark marketplace. A startled gay population began stumbling in, grabbing at one another in the gloom, and throwing punches at shadows. Today—well, fasten your seat belts. The horizon, it turns out, is no barrier at all, and thousands of fresh troops are scrambling past it every day.

You know all about this. You've heard stories, talked to friends, believed some of it, and laughed at the rest. Or maybe you've been there for a while, like me. You signed on years ago and began the circuit course of chats, messages, and ad interplay you had no idea would become the major, if not sole, avenue through which you would meet men. But the games are driving you crazy. You can't take one more liar, one more online stalker, one more tease. Hours spent in a chat room with no connection made. Again. You click yourself out, determined never to waste another night in front of a keyboard and a screen, surrounded by a sea of men who are not real.

Here's the thing, though: They are real. They're every one of them as real as you or I are, and most certainly as real as the men you used to look at, buy a drink for, or turn your back to in the bars. It's merely that we're all coming from a different place now. Yes, we're reaching out to find one another—for love, for a friend, for a half hour's kicks—in bigger numbers than ever before. But now we're doing it through a sometimes mysterious and frequently mischievous middleman: the

Internet, which gives us access to one another on a level so unprecedented, it dwarfs the invention of the printing press.

But a middleman can filter, just as it can connect. We're now talking to one another, quite literally, through boxes. What's said doesn't always translate faithfully; what's heard is liable to have undergone a shift in meaning by the time it has reached the other guy's ears. And as the language evolves, behavior itself follows, frantically trying to adapt. Small wonder millions of gay men pound millions of fists on computer desks, charge millions of dollars on thousands of new dating sites, and, far too often, spend millions of nights alone. The gay man online has become a rather old-fashioned paradigm: He is the diner starving at the feast.

He doesn't have to be. You sure don't. The varnish is still drying on the Internet, and the rules are evolving with every online session we log on to. Yet men looking for other men have managed to get together for thousands of years, and under some very adverse circumstances indeed. No need to let a little thing like the ultimate in access to one another stop us.

Read on, fellow user. If you're out there, he is too. All we have to do is get you connected.

THE BASICS

WHAT YOU'RE AFTER

FORGET FOR A MOMENT THAT THERE'S ANY SUCH ANIMAL as the Internet. You can do it; the cyberuniverse hasn't been around all *that* long, after all. Then think, for just that moment, of the way you go about getting the things you require to keep your life on track.

No need to get all abstract, here. This is about the fundamental stuff of our days, and that's all you need to conjure just now. Money comes in handy, and you get yourself a job for that regular paycheck. Food is a fairly reliable dependence, so it's safe to surmise that you shop for it, bring it home, and cook it, or sometimes have other people in restaurants do the dirty work for you. And when you crave a little entertainment, you probably take a trip to the movies. Or you subscribe to a DVD delivery service because that works better for you. The point being, in all these relatively ordinary pursuits, you pretty much *know what you need* and you take the necessary steps to obtain those things. No matter the object, you head for the sources best suited to your location, limits, tastes, and standards of quality.

7

Okay, let's bring the Internet back.

Millions of gay men turn to it as an important, if not primary, source of companionship. But, in a lapse they would never permit themselves in any other arena of their lives, they go in woefully unprepared. The same man who won't consider a trip to the mall without at least a general battle plan will, in his *search for someone important to him*, close his eyes, cross his fingers, and jump. This holds true for the guy who's after a casual good time as well. He knows he wants to get together with someone hot. But what that "hot" is, how hot it has to be for him to be interested enough, and even his own degree of want at the time—these are little things he generally expects the online experience to answer *for* him.

Each time you log on to chat with other men or to find one for more than chatting, you are the Internet. You make it what it is, for yourself and for all the men who come into contact with you. So the choice is yours, either to drift along, vaguely unsure of what you're there for, or to step in with confidence in what you have to offer and a strong sense of what would be satisfying to you. Yes, just as in any "real" gathering, the men you encounter will often dictate your behavior. An unexpectedly fun and clever chatter may soften that lusty ambition you went in with, just as a supremely hot guy interested in you might get you a little steamier than you had supposed you were. Fine. Reaction is the keynote when we mingle with others anywhere at all.

But by and large, you should know pretty clearly why

you're going in every time you do go in. Even if it's merely to hang out and see who else is hanging out, because that's a goal—albeit a modest one—in itself. The man who signs on with no intent other than hoping to see if, just maybe, someone fantastic is in there for him is the curse of gay online interaction. He's the same guy who spends his life waiting for something—or someone—to happen to him. It rarely does.

Again, moods change, even within a few minutes of one online session. Desires shift, intensity waxes and wanes. But your obligation to *know what you yourself are about* should be a constant. Go into cyberspace with the same, solid sense of yourself you carry with you anywhere else you go. The stronger your identity, and the more you know what works for you and what doesn't, the more likely you are to exit with that gratifying feeling you get from having met a new pal, or from setting in motion something potentially excellent. Or from just passing a very agreeable hour or two.

YOUR ONLINE IDENTITY

Who you gonna be today?
—"I'm Alright," Kenny Loggins

A GENTLEMAN ON TV THE OTHER DAY—TRUE STORY— was saying something highly compelling about the Internet. His point wasn't original, yet it wasn't one you come across every day.

He was talking about the online experience. And what he was utterly confounded by was that, in every single other setting of life, you are expected to be known as yourself. You use your real name. Always. In most situations it's nothing short of illegal to do otherwise. Yet online is different, as everybody knows and as he fumed about.

Only your Internet service provider (ISP) need know who you really are, and it calls for something on the order of a subpoena for them to divulge who you really are. Aren't they wonderful, those respectful and protective ISPs? Well, no. Obviously, they keep our secrets not to be good sports and real chums, but for business reasons. The ISP knows that when customers choose to use at least one fake identity online, it's because when under that name, they'd rather the rest of the

11

world not know who they really are. And a casual revealing of that information by any ISP would mean locking its doors and selling off its equipment in no time at all.

Of course, our friend on TV was right. We are raised to grow into taking responsibility for what we do *under our own name*, or we certainly should be. But it makes you wonder. How much of that noble instilling of personal responsibility for our actions would have been passed down from generation to generation had there been AOL back when Prohibition was mandated and flappers flapped? How much of this American forthrightness would exist—at least in cozy memory—if the wicked luxury of presenting yourself as anyone you pleased was available when our grandpappies were whittling?

Less. For we have all learned to accept the consequences of what we do primarily because there was never before an alternative. No, that's not to say that the decency around us today is wholly dependent on accountability. But remember, this isn't about grabbing cash from a bank teller. This isn't the realm of active and harmful crime. This is about introductions, chatting, cruising, dating, and a lot of make-believe, all between consenting grown-ups. So the indulgence of fraudulent personal representation is, all things considered, tame. Widespread, but tame.

Yes, there are those who use the Internet for a host of wrong reasons, or just plain criminal reasons. They make the papers every day. The good news, though, is that they *do* make the papers. The better news is that more and more of them are getting caught and making the first editions every day, as online users increasingly learn how to protect themselves, their bank info, and their families.

As for the rest of us, it's pretty simple. Facing reality is the ticket here. An oxymoronic ticket, given the subject at hand, but the ticket all the same. As long as the option exists to sail along online under an assumed name, people will do a great deal of it. But that's really quite all right. Provided the using public understands the game—and the using public has no excuse not to, by now—the playing field is level. It's a bit like the age-old battle about censorship, and who is entitled to decide what is and isn't dirty. One may not always be able to say with certainty what pornography isn't, but it's far easier to recognize it as it is. And if you truly believe that Hung9Stud2Dewu—*under that particular screen name*, for he may in fact be your insurance agent when cooled down and otherwise designated—is this fellow's primary identity in the world, the least of your problems is online intercourse.

Here's a basic identity suggestion: follow the path forged by Hung and the millions like our lusty insurance peddler. Employ two names for your online traffic. One for the north of the waistline, the other for the south. Enhancing the more lowbrow name with bolder color, different graphics, and anything short of a boxing referee's bell that can be added to it is a good idea as well. This is strongly recommended as a safeguard if you dabble in dual names at all.

The savviest user has momentarily dropped his guard and e-mailed a business acquaintance from his cruising screen name. It can easily happen, as many similar heart-stopping errors have happened.

Take the hypothetical case of a gentleman known online—some of the time, anyway—as SukUOffNow. He was playing around online, he remembered a business contact he had to make, and so he made it. Without switching back to his mainstream identity. Then he saw his error, and then he broke out in a cold sweat.

Suk's lot was not a happy one. For a brief moment in which hope pulsed, he seized upon the likelihood of the recipient's eyeing the smutty name and summarily disposing of the thing as spam, unread. Regrettably, Suk had been a tad too specific about the business matter in his subject heading. Furthermore, our friend Suk could not "unsend" the perfidious note; he used AOL, you see, and only AOL e-mails to other AOL users may be so aborted. . . .

Don't let this happen to you. It only takes a half second to slip, and it's far too easy to click send and trust to your usual good sense. Always, *always* take that precious moment to stop and double-check who you are and to whom you are writing. In no time, it'll become a habit.

Now, let's get to business: the name you choose for your cruising/dating alter ego.

Below are cautions and suggestions for the name you will compose for yourself. The master name you employ, the respectable one you are careful to keep distinct from the randy one, is probably going to be a simple spelling of your real name or a combination of that and your locale. There isn't much of a call for esoteric advice here; you know how to tie your own necktie. As elsewhere in this guide, the roads traveled are a little gritty, and free of formal wear.

Also, don't let an eager ISP or your own state of excitement about going online rush you. Toss a few ideas back and forth, let them marinate awhile in your head or on a piece of paper. It's just a screen name, sure, and it's probably one you can drop or edit as you please. But we men are lazy. We wear the same threadbare shorts until they decompose, and we stick to a dumb name because we can't be bothered to change it.

Most important, think about what your screen names are *for*. Your basic, all-purpose, business and/or social screen name is an ID, plain and simple, created to serve you in your interactions with friends, family, and colleagues. But the alternate name, the dating and cruising name, calls for some thought. Is it hot sex with strangers you're after, and that's it? Okay, go wild. Getting an interesting man interested in you, without initially revealing who you are? Lower the heat.

No, it isn't easy. But remember that taking the middle road is usually the best, and safest. You can always get either nastier or more sentimental when the actual communicating happens. Present the basic facts about yourself, add a little personality-driven shading, and there's no forum, no online pursuit, you won't be able to happily navigate.

Below are some common pitfalls to resist:

• Avoid the word "boy." Even if that is what, technically, you are. For one thing, it appears that every possible name permutation incorporating it has been used. Which leaves you "boi." Which is also everywhere, irritating, and disturbingly evocative of food paste from Hawaii. Add "boi" to your name if you are twenty-five or older, and fully expect to be regarded online as an actress from the Ziegfeld Follies days trying to pass herself off as thirtyish with the aid of dim light and rubber bands under the chin.

If you nonetheless insist that, as a nineteen-year-old surfer, you are supremely entitled to use "boi," I cannot stop you. Go right ahead. You would not respond to my IMs, anyway.

• On a related note, still very much alive and kicking is "dude." Some slang can live a long and healthy life. This is rare, however, as slang is intrinsically born of the moment and fated to die soon after. "Dude" is survivor slang. It lives on but has had to adapt into a sarcastic version of its former coolness. You can indeed say "dude." But *only* in a tongue-in-cheek way. If you can work a self-effacing "dude" into your screen name, more power to you. Just know that it won't be easy. And "dood" or "dewd" is just plain painful.

- It isn't an especially good idea to insert your age in your screen name. Remember that time marches on, and you *still* won't throw those shorts away.

- Long strings of numbers, however meaningful they may be to you, are a pain in the ass. Many of us are not good with cutting-and-pasting into an e-mail or IM. Your name should be easy, likable, steamy, memorable, genuinely fun—all of these, or at least one of these. It should not look like a formula in quantum physics.

- If you can invent a variation on "hung," "stud," "buff," "gym," or "jock" that has yet to be taken, your immense talents are wasted online.

- A hitherto unseen mix-and-match of the aforementioned abused adjectives and nouns may still be possible. After all, millions of songs comprise the same meager number of available notes. But resist the temptation. All that will ensue is overkill; by the time the other user gets to your fourth descriptive, dripping-with-testosterone descriptive word, it is all lost. Besides, inch differences in pec dimensions notwithstanding, it is just too easy to confuse "gymjockhungbuffdude" with "jockgymstudhungnbuff."

And, hung buff jock stud that you are, you deserve to stand alone, don't you?

• Conceivably, it's a good idea to squeeze in a clue to your general location (depending, of course, on what you're after). If you go under this name merely for gratification through interaction, then there's no point. But if at least some of the time you're cruising to meet up with a man—or even fall in love—then yes.

It may be your state's initials, or the first key letters of the metropolis you call home, as in "ATL" or "CHI." Either way, try to weave something of this information into your name if it suits your purposes. This will also help screen you from more geographically focused, and less hot, attentions.

• Try to steer clear of *excessive* cuteness, the name that's constructed in such a way that the joke of it is known only through the actual saying of it, e.g., "DixieMense." Cuteness, like a smolderingly sexy name, is an extreme of sorts, and you won't always be feeling just that way online. You'll have plenty of opportunity to show how charming and funny you can be when conversing. But the name that's a little too cryptic is no good; it turns people off, no matter how much work you put into the cleverness.

• Along the lines of multiple numbers, again: Take the trouble to have a good look at the name you're tinkering with before you set it in stone. We all need to drop a vowel here and there in order to employ those too-employed key words. Understood. Yet there is no excuse for a mess like "BUFMSCLHTJCK." If your every attempt at creating a clearer version of such a name is rejected as having been taken, simply insert the name Fred into it. Fred is a nice, manly name.

- Let's say you truly are "jockmusclebuffgymstud," vowels and all. Cheers. And hearty congratulations for having nailed the name. But please, *please*—refrain from adding a "4U" to the end of it. Even if those two characters are what secures the name as your own. For the sad fact is, those intensely alluring names terminating in "4U" are rarely, if ever, 4 anyone at all. This ostensibly generous tag invariably bookends the screen identities of those men who don't—as a rule—give much up.

- It is not easy for a man of a certain age to comprehend, but young men come to online cruising with a different perspective, and with a lot less shame, guilt, and/or baggage. Hence the one-name-for-all activity. They think of themselves as integrated beings, soulful *and* hot, clever *and* buff. With all the fierce pride of the young warrior, they see no reason to conduct online affairs of the crotch as anyone but who they are to the world (as long as the BF (or GF) is gone for the weekend, anyway). If you yourself are young, I salute your bravery. If you are not young, don't fume. They'll learn. The cruising alter ego isn't even about shame; it's about taking care of *all* the business in your life without going mad.

• You're in a chat because you're looking. This is understood by everyone else in the online chat/dating galaxy. In fact, it's a safe assumption that every single person jammed into every single chat room is—that's right—looking. Adding to your screen name a verb form to indicate a searching mode—the classic "iso," or "in search of"—is like waving a match from the top of a lighthouse.

• Remembering again that your intentions, noble or animal, can be conveyed through your online conversing, consider going the route of the simple, regular *name*. Mike, or Mike777. Robert, or ElPasoRob. The Internet has changed a great deal of how we view the world and what we expect from it, but one thing remains consistently true: Simplicity is attractive.

Ultimately, what you want your screen name to reflect is a self-assured, nonspecific *presence*. You are different people at different times of day. Too many gay men, in the heat of the moment, select a screen name that conveys a degree of erotic or romantic intensity they feel only sporadically. This creates confusion when they merely want to chat amiably with a fellow user. Here, as elsewhere in life, it's wise to recall that the man you are in the literal world, walking out the door every morning, is open to myriad possibilities. In real life, your first name works just fine as an initial gateway to the many and diverse things you are seeking and have to offer. Let it serve you as efficiently in the cybergalaxy.

YOUR ONLINE PROFILE

EVERY MAJOR ISP ALLOWS YOU TO CREATE A PROFILE FOR yourself, a one-page résumé of who you are and what you find interesting. This is your introduction to the millions who want an idea of what you're all about. And, in the world of gay chat rooms and dating, this is your calling card to the guy you most definitely want to get to know better.

All right, then. All a guy has to do is jot down a few lines, relay a few enticing basic facts about his physicality, maybe indicate the sort of man he's most attracted to, and click save.

Easy, yes? You would think. But what men *do*, and *do,* and *do*, is knock themselves out in feeble attempts to come across as clever, insightful, poetic, romantically disarming, sensitive, brilliant, tougher than leather, passionate, obscurely hip, or any combination thereof. It is frightening. You can almost see the drops of sweat that fell as these insanely ambitious self-tributes were composed. All that work, all that self-promotion, and for nothing. Most certainly for nothing, when the object is to actually draw a man to themselves.

When most gay men are in a cruising or romantic state of mind and simultaneously facing a blank profile page, they overcompensate like nobody's business. They defeat their purpose by bellowing the ordinary, by rudely demanding what in real life they would merely request, and by digging up and revealing real or imagined aspects of themselves no one but a life partner of many years' duration should know about.

REALITY CHECK

The profile is a simple introductory page. Always be honest, be a little hot and a little charming when you can, then get out. To go beyond this, as so many users so vigorously and sometimes hysterically do, is asking for trouble. It is assuredly not asking for company. The too commonly seen gay profile, baring soul and heartache and demand/need, is the cyber equivalent to wanting to stop by your favorite bar for a drink and maybe meet up with a hot guy, but only after stopping home first to change into a high-backed Renaissance collar, a sequined thong, and nothing else. In a highly understated word, it is trying too damn hard.

Remember that you are creating a simple online profile. You are not Flaubert. You are not James Joyce. Nor are you commissioned by a major publisher to write your memoir.

Bear in mind what you already know from real life: *Whatever you are cannot be decently represented in a minute or two.* (Well, hopefully, anyway.) If you are at all interesting, you should be smart. If you're smart, you should know that adolescent drivel about the meaning of life doesn't attract anyone except the very desperate.

The same goes for writing long paragraphs in your profile about your romantic dreams. Attractive people in real life as we know it fly like bats out of hell at the first glimpse of anyone crying the blues about love. Should you take this avenue, be advised that no one, and I mean absolutely no one, is going to read more than a few lines of your epic. Online cruisers, whether old hands at the game or fresh recruits off the bus, all have excellent noses for self-important asses or pompous bores. Pseudopoetry about your soul and the moon can be spotted in the half second it takes to move the mouse to the upper right corner and click it off to the Great Cyber Landfill.

Never lose sight of just who your online audience is. See them in your head. They are not darkly good-looking and deeply soulful, trying one last time to find that profound, spiritual partner. They are all those average men you ever saw in adjacent cars at stoplights and all those few, compelling guys you sat next to on a plane. Most of all, they are, each and every one, just as entitled to sex and/or love as you are, just as certain that they deserve the best, and just as doubtful as to how worthy of their company—for an hour or forever—you yourself are.

So how *do* you draw quality people to you who have in mind more than just fast sex, a quickie with an online stranger? A few well-chosen words about how hot your ass is will get them talking. That's glib, of course. But it isn't entirely a joke. You must incorporate some sense of your physicality into your profile, and it should be attractive. When we stop and do a double-take on the street after a good-looking guy passes, it isn't because we have an uncanny feeling that he is a fascinating person. We want to get near him because he's appealing; let the rest unfold as it will, and hopefully on the side of a captivating interior.

Online, the cart is pulling the horse. You're out to get that double-take before he's seen you. Even if your profile page permits photo display, that enticement is still a click away, and he has to want to click. So, in the basic ISP profile, you have to rely on the proven draws of the nonvisual. Think engaging, think clear, think honest. Think—and you'll see this again shortly because it's the keystone of the whole process—of what would make *you* look twice, click on a picture link, or start a conversation.

REALITY CHECK

The person looking over your profile is interested in one thing, and one thing only: what you look like. Make no mistake about this. Yes, he will claim otherwise. But when he makes contact, it is only because he has already assumed you are hot stuff.

Lastly, and too frequently unconsidered, *be in the right frame of mind* when you sit down to compose this profile. Be feeling good about yourself, about life, about the world. Depend upon it: This will be reflected in what you write about yourself and your situation. It isn't magic; it's the way of humankind, in that how we are at the moment is carried over into whatever occupation we're engaged in. Since the profile is your handshake to millions, let it be nice, firm, and coming from a man with no axes to grind.

Very often, however, knowing what *not* to do is more effective than hearing about what you ought to do. Let's delve, then, into specific profile pitfalls. Heed the warnings, and succeed. Ignore, and . . . well, there's always porn.

- Don't steal. Don't copy. One of the first and best profiles I ever read made its debut through America Online back in 1996. Under the space for a favorite quote was written: "I want to die in my sleep like my grandfather, and not like the screaming passengers in his car." Clever? You bet. A week later, however, the same gag popped up in another profile. Within three weeks clumsy variations of it sprouted up everywhere. While there's a strong case for the old saw, "talent creates, genius steals," it's a shame that the joke's pioneer will never be known. And the joke itself isn't seen as funny at all once the mass circulating begins; it's seen as stolen. Far, far better to be maybe less funny, but your original self.

- Do you like "fun"? Is it something you enjoy having? You've hit the jackpot, then, because everyone else online likes it too. Many, in fact, take the trouble to add this inclination to their profiles, as though to stun and shock all those who positively hate fun. *Do not be one of them.*

- Just as a fondness for fun need not be advertised, you can take it on good faith that there are others out there who like movies. And music. It's not an especially risky bet, in fact, that most anyone you hook up with online will turn out to enjoy movies *and* music, should your encounter evolve at all beyond groping. Telling the world that you like movies and music is like telling Jessica Simpson to smile more often. It isn't necessary.

- If you believe that you must share the hoary inspiration that "Life is short!", then it is already way too long.

- Any aphorism that may well be seen below a calendar picture of a kitten dangling by its paws, on an oversize coffee mug, or stuck to your mom's refrigerator door doesn't belong in a profile.

- Amendment to above: No aphorism is good. They are uniformly preachy and smug. Do not fill profile space with them.

- If you wish to leave the name line blank, do so. There is no need to add a combative/bitchy remark about why you are opting for anonymity. No one at all is wondering. Really, they're not.

- Don't ever use your *full* real name. Not in the world of gay online dating, anyway. It isn't that you're setting yourself up for potential and very three-dimensional trouble, although you are; it's more that you're also opening wide the real-life door to who you are—and subsequently how you can be tracked down—to every Internet peddler of everything from stocks to Viagra.

- If your real first name is, through no fault of your own, hopelessly bizarre, don't use it. Use the nickname that's been salvaged from it in your real life.

- Employing a fake first name—when there's really no need, given how the real one can't hurt you—won't do much to impress those guys to whom you later want to reveal the truth. That hot man is probably seriously going to wonder why on earth you felt the need to call yourself Bob online when your name, it turns out, is David. Forget mistrust and subterfuge; it just doesn't point to a great deal of intelligence.

- Don't shoot for cleverness in your profile if the result isn't unquestionably clever *and* understandable. For one thing, another profile already has that devastating observation within it. For another, cleverness is usually not hot.

- If you announce that you are searching for an LTR (long-term relationship), you are not doomed. You are already buried. Even the most ardent Oprah fan knows that genuinely enriching companionship isn't had by asking for it. Add this yearning to your profile and you need never worry again about tweezing those nose hairs.

REALITY CHECK

The Murphy's Law of profiles: expressed need = increased personal space. The more urgently the need expressed, the greater the personal space given.

- Spell correctly. It isn't that hard. If it is, take advantage of the free dictionaries found exactly where you're setting down this profile: online.

Sure, even the best of us slip up. It's hard not to slip up in a frenzied IM conversation. But a profile is different. It's your baby, and you've got plenty of time to groom it properly. The numbers of people who indulge in childishly poor spelling and grammar in this arena are astronomical. And bad—often appalling—grammar and spelling doesn't go very far in promoting the writer's goal of being seen as smart and together, as so many of us wish to be seen.

For example, the writer of "Life's too short!" is clearly a guy who isn't particularly bothered by any demons of originality.

All right, that's his call. But the writer of "Lifes to short!" is downright scary. Life may be relatively brief, but it doesn't take very long to master "to," "too," and—God help us—"two."

> The embellishing of what you do for a living is shot to hell by your own poor spelling. That is, it's hard to accept that anyone who refers to his career as "financal maneger" is enjoying a corner office at Citibank.

> Your profile can be accessed and changed at any given minute, 24/7. In fact, this may be the one feature just about every ISP blows itself away on, for each edit is followed by the advisement that the changes will be visible within a day, and yet are up instantaneously. So there is no excuse whatsoever for not checking your handiwork for errors.

> As basic as it gets: When in doubt, look it up. If you're a poor speller, don't wait for the doubt.

> Note: The single exception to the correct spelling protocol is the bimbo. If you are billing yourself as an extremely sexy guy, gifted with an enormous appetite for sex and a body you see less as a temple for your spirit and more as a ripped or stacked background location to central points of orgasm, and if only these nasty aspects and attributes are what you are sharing with America, okay. Spell any way you want. It's hotter if you're stupid.

- dON't tyPe lIkE thIZZ on-LeZ UR 12 r yUnG'R.

- Brevity is what we're after, yes. But nothingness is carrying it a little far, as in the completely blank profile page. It may have been interesting once, back in 1994, when someone first practiced this cyber nihilism. Even then, it was interesting for about a second and a half.

     Everyone likes to leave a certain degree of mystery about himself. Absolutely. But it is arrogance of a very high order to expect anyone to want to fill in *all* the blanks. Ultimately, the vacant profile page feels like an unfunny prank because that is precisely what it is.

- AOL is the culprit that first added the option of the personal quote to the profile setup. Presumably, the intent was to let the user share his life's motto with the world, and they clearly pushed a very popular button with this one. Virtually every ISP now provides the user plenty of space for one.

     Leave it alone. Presidential candidates and Boy Scouts are the only two groups who should have a slogan at the ready, and my sincere hope is that neither of these collectives does a lot of online cruising.

- If you *must* set down a quote, write it in French, Italian, or German. You will offend few with the opinion or feeling it relates because almost no one will understand it, and they will think it is pretty cool and wise.

- Do not quote Madonna in your profile.

- Do not quote Cher. Even Cher knows better than to do that.

- Don't quote Emerson in your profile and then go into a sex chat room. Emerson deserves better, if Cher doesn't.

- AOL's profile form now asks you to name your favorite gadgets. It is utterly incomprehensible that someone with authority in the AOL offices did not slam a heavy foot down on this one, and fast. There is only so much suspension of disbelief even a vast corporate entity can engage in; they had to know they were asking for it. Moreover, anyone at all would have thought that the zillion brutal responses to its "computer" query might have steered them away from such easily mocked territory.

  Anyway, *do not* write "The one in my hand!" Do not write "It's 8 inches and hard!" Do not in any manner refer to your genitalia by way of response to this question. This is the space in which to get specific about whom you want to have sex with. Use the "hobbies" or "occupation" space to set down your size and stamina.

- Much has been made about the AOL, or online, yardstick as opposed to real measurements when it comes to the length and girth of the male organ as described by its owner. In fact, "AOL inches" has slyly slipped into our vernacular and collective consciousness, much as "friendly fire" and other such phrases have been digested.

This presents a problem for someone writing a profile, no matter which ISP he uses. Because in a market full of size queens, size is king. How, then, to be honest in a world where everyone else is adding two inches? Let's say you are 7, and you write "7." Everyone will think you are 5, won't they?

Well, yes and no. It is very much a no-win scenario. But there are acceptable guidelines and they are, not surprisingly, dependent on the inches themselves:

If you are 5 or under, you really need to say so. But add that you are extremely thick. Thickness compensates for length quite nicely in the fevered minds of the profile cruiser. If you are not—sorry, but you have no choice but to be completely honest. You have to say, "I have a small dick." But to a guy interested in you, *that is not the end of the world.* Seriously. Here, as elsewhere, this handicap can be overcome by other attractions, not the least of which is a genuinely cool, breezy acceptance of the smallness of your own size.

If you are 6, 7, or 8, relax. You're being waved in.

9 and over . . . this is tricky territory. Attach a picture (you have no alternative, making this claim), and be sure the photo can't be taken as one pulled from an amateurs' gallery. Tag it with a watermark.

Should you sport an appendage of 10, 11, or 12 inches, see the above. Even then, you and it will be doubted. There is no way around this. Just post the watermarked picture, ignore the nonbelievers, and move on. And everyone who

contacts you—there will be contacts, depend upon it—
has been properly warned.

Before you send your profile out into the cold, hard
cyberworld, take a moment to review. Yes, you can change it
whenever you like. But starting out strong is a sound policy
for everything from corporate takeovers to sack races. I tend to
think romance is no exception.

Don't forget, either, the laziness of the average male.
Specifically, yours. It's a cliché and a peculiar thing, but valid
nonetheless: Men will invest many hours, weeks, months, and
dollars in seeking out sex or love, or both, online. They will
do this knowing, somewhere in their minds, that their profiles
aren't quite what they could be. But they will not change them.
The Decomposing Undershorts Syndrome strikes again.

So, a checklist for your completed online profile:

✓ First and foremost, open the profile and *see* it before you
read it. Is the amount of actual copy in any way off-putting?
Because if it doesn't look to be a fast read, it's too wordy.

If length is an issue, edit. Cut. Slash. The best writers
in the world have had to "kill their darlings" for the greater
good of the work; you can certainly delete the tired line
about waiting to see what happens if you hit it off.

✓ Get into the mind-set of the guy you're trying to attract.
Meditate if you must, channel if you can, but do it. Then

read your profile. If you don't find yourself wanting to know more, you've said far too much.

✓ Are your physical dimensions in there, and honestly so? Age, weight, build—all of it? If not, add them. If fudged, unfudge. If the idea is to actually meet up with someone, they will know you played with the truth if not beat it up altogether. Profile deception in regard to physicality is responsible for more slammed doors and more two-minute coffeehouse meetings than all the blind dates ever misguidedly arranged combined.

✓ Check your spelling. Trust me.

✓ If you opted to go with unique punctuation—e.g., everything in lowercase letters—that's all right. But keep it uniform. A "typo" here explodes the cool you were out to achieve.

✓ Kill any emoticons whatsoever. Then smack yourself for having inserted them in the first place.

✓ Ditto aphorisms, one-liners, and similar space wasters.

✓ If you intend to use your profile to reel in men from chats, is your willingness or nonwillingness to date evident? Think about the men who'll be reading it. Does it broadcast that you're available, maybe *too* available, when you'd really rather leave that possibility for later?

✓ What's the *feel*? Brevity and honest, straightforward facts are what you want, to be sure. But also your end product should come across as confident, assured, and, yes, *nice*.

Let's now have a gander at a few example profiles. Tips are great. Advice is fine. But nothing imparts the reality of a task like seeing a version or two in action.

Oh, you've already seen your share of profiles, you think. No doubt you have; we all have, and quite a bit more than our share too. The thing is, though, you've also already forgotten just about every one of them. Which is exactly why you need to look again, and with the eyes of a man who isn't about to join those forgettable ranks.

No single profile is going to attract everyone. You don't want that, anyway. But this is, in a very real sense, a résumé you're sending out to the dating world. And there are all too common errors that may well lose you the interest of the ones you *do* want to attract.

Name: Barry
Location: Raleigh, NC (Go, Razorbacks!!!!)
Marital Status: NO!!!
Computer: WHY IS THIS QUESTION HERE???
Occupation: Health care
Hobbies and Interests: Dinning, dancing, being with friends is GREAT, love all kinds of music.
Heres what you really want to know—I am 5'8", 170

lbs, average build but cute (they say, anyway!) Looking
for LTR but in the mean time like fun!!!
Personal Quote: do you believe in life after love . . . ??

What is Barry actually telling us about himself? What's
the vibe?

For better or worse, Barry appears to be fairly
stereotypical. He either doesn't know or doesn't care that
he's presenting himself as exceptionally ordinary. His sense
of humor is feeble at best (the "computer" answer and
the qualifier to his cuteness); he quotes Cher, which is as
stereotypically gay as you can get since Liberace passed on;
he's insecure (there's neediness in the emphatic extolling of
his social life and in that "like fun!!!"), and we don't believe
for a second that Barry gives it up for the Razorbacks; and
very basic spelling and grammar errors point to an overall
messiness in his persona.

Name: DCCop4u
Location: figure it out
Marital Status: was
Occupation: figure it out
Personal Quote: spread em

Now, the novice may see this profile and lose no time in
messaging this officer. In the gay world, cops tend to be a hot
commodity. Also, he transmits the rough terseness associated

with a he-man. He has no time for capital letters. Hell, he has no time for periods.

But look twice; there's a lot wrong here. First, most real police officers don't announce their occupations in profiles circulating in gay chats. He may well be one, but it's smart not to take this on faith, at least not right away.

Second, why has our cop not set down his age or physical attributes? Hmm. Hot guys usually do, you know. The online officer who does not make much of his body is, more often than not, the officer with a belly. And, as policemen are ordinarily slow to divorce, we can surmise that he is of a certain age. Certainly not a young one.

All told, the profile above raises more than one red flag.

Name: Mike
Location: Tulsa
Marital Status: yeah
Occupation: landscaper
Hobbies and Interests: 28 5 10 work out 46 chst 30 wst 16 bis

Well done, Mike.

Note the beautiful simplicity, the almost Japanese sparseness to his profile. Mike has wisely chosen not to answer those queries he finds unnecessary; this is admirable and, in this domain, indicates some serious self-control. Note too the name Mike, rather than Michael. Mike does not need to tell us he is a masculine kind of man—it's there for anyone to see.

But the biggest thing Mike is telegraphing is ambiguity. And it resides in those physical stats. Yep, they're impressive. But the fact that this extremely curt, seemingly straight guy is both aware of his exact dimensions and glad to post them indicates some arrogance—which can be a turn-on—and very possibly a mixed-up notion of his own sexuality.

> **Name:** Jeff, J to my friends, Jeffrey to MY MOTHER, oh, hell, call me anything, I'll come LOL
> **Location:** San Francisco. HAD to be here, it's where I left my heart. . . .
> **Marital Status:** Well I'm still waiting for my prince. But you have to kiss a LOT of frogs first!
> **Occupation:** Medical field
> **Favorite Gadget:** I think YOU have it, not me LOL
> **Hobbies and Interests:** Is anyone real anymore? Why is it so hard to find someone with an open heart and a mind ready to see new things, experience what another soul has to give? You will not now love until your willing to give it.

This is just plain bad news.

What's screamingly apparent in this profile is . . . well, the screaming. Jeff clearly thinks he's a riot, when in fact each stab at humor ("kiss a LOT of frogs," the "gadget" remark) is downright awful. It gets worse, too; the pining at the close is simultaneously egotistical (*he's* ready, the world isn't), pocked with errors and frantically desperate.

After reading this online, you'd do well to think twice before even going near San Francisco.

The profile scene. It's a hoot, isn't it?

No. It's a tool, and that's all it is. It's also a smart tool, because it lets you know if it's working or not. And if your own profile—despite your following all the advice given here, and there's no question you have faithfully—is lying around in cyberspace attracting nothing but cobwebs, it's time to revamp.

Which is fine. Thanks to the traffic and the magic of the Web, every hour begins a brand-new day, and largely a spanking-new world, on the Internet.

YOUR PICTURES ONLINE: THE GOOD, THE BAD . . .

LONG, LONG AGO, AROUND THE EARLY NINETIES, FEW were the online users who had photographs of themselves to share with other users. The concept and the technology were still new and daring. No one felt comfortable with it because too few were doing it. Once everyone jumps into the water, however—and it is a very crowded baptismal pool out there today—there is no one left on shore to yell that you look ridiculous and really should put something on.

REALITY CHECK

The online cruiser/dater without a picture of himself to send is the hunter without gun or machete. He may survive in the jungle. He may even miraculously find something on which to feast. But the smart money isn't on him. You need a photo of yourself to send to other interested men, or there will be very, very few interested men.

These days just about all of us share photographs online. We share them like a maniacal grandmother with a box full of picture albums. Myspace.com—not a bad avenue for meeting somebody, if not *everybody*, out there—grows by leaps and bounds daily, and a major draw is the unlimited picture art you can post. No matter how sensational the copy, the Internet is and will always be a visually reliant medium. What's presented doesn't have to dance. But people want to see it.

There are two sorts of pictures the equipped user ought to have in a file and at his disposal to send. You very likely have several of one kind already: snaps of you and the dog, you and the car, you and the Leaning Tower of Pisa. These are your Norman Rockwells, your wholesome, safe shots, usually referred to as your G-rated pics. The ones NetZero and AOL shamelessly hawk in their noble quest to remind the American youth that he has grandparents and that they live to see snaps of him clowning around at the pool. These are the shots friends have sent to your hard drive after that lousy vacation you spent with them, or the pics you yourself wanted, to commemorate that visit to Yosemite or that drunken birthday bash with the guys. The respectable ones. These you have. Half the battle is done.

One catch. Sort of.

There is such a thing as *too* respectable, if your aim is to attract a sexual partner. A suit is no good. Too much is hidden. And the picture of you on a lounge chair, the one

If you look sensational in that picture taken at Christmas, with Mom and Sis on either side of you, then by all means use that picture. But crop it, removing Mom and Sis. It is easy to do with the photo options available on Windows and Mac systems; go to "My Pictures" and follow the edit instructions. Essentially, you drag your mouse over the portion of the photo you would like to extract, and then right-click and save it under a new name in whatever folder you'd like to keep it in.

Cropping is important because seeing your mother is not conducive to the sexual energy that exciting man would like to develop with you. Besides, it's your *mother*, for heaven's sake.

where just your collarbone and above is exposed, is downright cheating. Face is great. We all like to see a handsome one, and if handsome is what you are, excellent. But no single gay man on the prowl online is content to see only that. By all means, use your good "face pic" to get his attention. Just be sure to have the clear body shot to send after, to reel him in.

So too are group shots bad news here; your caption of "I'm the second one on the right!" to distinguish the little that can be made out of you from the crowd will serve only to irritate that guy who was intrigued by your profile. Or worse, get him interested in your cousin to the left, or your younger brother just behind your shoulder. Which, it's a pretty safe bet, wasn't your goal when you sent the picture.

You also run a risk with the classic drunk-party picture by revealing your party animal persona. If the shot shows you off as hot and if a good time is all you're after with the recipient, terrific. But it's not a picture to reveal to someone you just might want to develop something with, thus it shouldn't be readily available to anyone who can access your profile pictures.

John was eager to meet Mike after Mike sent him a picture of himself and his buddies on a spring break excursion. Mike was cute, no doubt about it, and John was a little in love in no time at all. But the friend to Mike's left was cuter. The friend was in fact a *roommate* of Mike's as well, and these two factors played a sizable role in John's attraction. He did not actually acknowledge it at the time, but what he was doing was setting himself up to meet what he wanted more.

Unfortunately, it turned out that the roomie was straight. Even more unfortunately, the roomie was days away from marriage. And John, gleaning all of this, had to face the reality of not really having liked Mike all that much to begin with. In fact, with the roomie utterly unavailable, Mike's attractions were rendered zero. All of which made Mike rethink his deliberate and self-defeating strategy of displaying himself with better-looking friends.

Ultimately, if you are playing the game and playing it fairly, you need the in-between picture. A little more smoldering than the Norman Rockwell and a good bit less bold than your nude, it should reveal enough for the viewer—who is, after all, a man you are trying to attract—to fill in any gaps. The shot of you grinning stupidly with one arm around your fat cousin at a wedding isn't going to do it. The one of you washing the car or the shot of you taking a breather on a hike might. Nothing too studied is desired here, nothing too deliberately casual. Yet bare-chested or in a polo shirt, at the beach or on a bridge, the picture must present you with your maleness up front and a decent sense of your body's proportions on the table. If your profile indicates a healthy degree of athleticism, then the picture you send out should be shirtless, or the shirt should be very snug indeed.

REALITY CHECK

If you categorize yourself as a man's man, then the photo should be sexy and the clothing minimal. This is not the picture to elicit "Hey, that looks like a nice guy," but rather "*Whoa*—now, that's a hot guy."

So the very best option, all things considered, is the summer shorts photo. It's respectable, plenty of skin is exposed, and risk is a nonissue. The picture can't compromise you because there's nothing at all wrong with the picture. And just as at the beach where the shot was taken, you encourage some fun wondering about the little that isn't bared.

What, incidentally, about the issue of safety? After all, in a little bitter irony, the very thing that makes any of those "safe" pictures safe also renders them hazardous. For they are the public you, and must be employed with extreme discretion when stalking game in a sexually oriented chat.

There is, of course, no shame or peril in trading G-rated pictures. What makes you send them is your affair; everyone is online with photos of themselves anyway, and a G-rated pic can never be used against you. But a sexually driven chat is inherently a different beast; the respectable photo you trade here is safe, but you aren't. You are allowing at least one person to know that there is a sexually predatory you under the suit or shorts. And even the otherwise cozy safeguard of living in a huge city, and thus being more confident of going unidentified, may not avail you here. If the online world has taught us anything, it is that the real world is quite as small as everyone always said it was. You may think it nigh well impossible that you will be spotted as that Allstate agent by a hot gentleman in NYCM4M or ATLANTAMUSC4MUSC. It happens.

But don't be afraid. Yes, it seems an extraordinary conundrum—how safely can you reveal yourself, and search for sex or a date, in a virtual room filled with your neighbors?—but the answer is logical, if disheartening. Here, as in other jungles, there is safety in numbers. The bigger the city in whose chat room you cruise, the more remote the chance of being identified as who you truly are, dressed and taking a meeting. And the truth is that the vast majority of those cruising, even in our nation's smallest hamlets, will not know you. Our neighbors are strangers to us. Today's world is isolationist; by all means, take advantage of it.

Also, generally speaking, an honor-among-thieves mentality holds sway in any M4M room. It is just plain bad form to call someone out on who he truly is, either in an IM or—unspeakably!—within the dialogue screen, and it is almost never done. As with our pre-Internet ancestors and their supposedly better characters, however, it is not necessarily fine moral fiber behind this civility. It is more why thieves occasionally protect one another—they don't want anyone singing on them.

Moreover, you are probably in no danger at all, even if someone is suddenly threatening to shatter your world. There are, sadly, cruisers out there who somehow think that hinting at blackmail is a sure way to get into someone's pants. That is, you may be approached by someone you are interested in. You trade G-rated pictures. His disappoints you, and you gently rebuff. Then comes the message "Don't I know you?" You panic. You suddenly envision the next day as a series of snickers in the office and sneers on the street.

Calm yourself, friend. As a modern psychologist will tell

you, those who would prey upon your anxieties have only as much power as you give them. Remember, too, that your would-be exposer is just as at risk. Call the bastard's bluff with a laid-back attitude. You know me? Great. Who cares? I sure don't. This diffuses the bomb, and the terrorist slinks away.

Finally, I hope there is little need to spell out the painfully obvious: If you work for a particularly sensitive branch of the government, if you are a member of the clergy (and I certainly hope you are not), or if you live in any other way that would be threatened or live with any person who would be hurt by your exposure as an online seeker of sex, be exceedingly careful. It may be best in these cases to do without pictures altogether, and take your chances in the jungle with only your fingernails and determination to rely on. It's rougher, but it isn't impossible.

. . . AND THE NAKED

Shake it, shake it like a Polaroid picture.
—"Hey ya!" OutKast

ON TO THE NEXT KIND OF PHOTO.

Do I really need to explain? This picture is the one that displays your naked body and/or genitalia, and is exceedingly useful in the arsenal of the guy who's after, if only now and then, an online hookup. It is the kind of picture you tuck into the most remote file of your hard drive or—better still, if your home is treacherously occupied by noncruising relations—keep only on a CD or disk stashed in the bottom of the sock drawer.

Here are the things you should know about this bold expression of your outer being:

• Do not—and I mean *do not*—attempt to pass off a photo stolen from an amateur gay website as your own. There is no single one of these that has not been seen and appreciated by millions already. Or else there is a certain marine cadet out there who has, à la Dorian Gray, not aged a day since

51

1994. The preservation is all the more remarkable, as he has also undergone the stress of moving to at least thirty major and minor cities in that time.

- Match collar and cuffs. That is to say, do not describe yourself in such a way that the photo you offer belies your statistics. This is especially true of gentlemen above a certain age. There are far too many pictures of men profiled as being in their forties who look like they waved good-bye to forty a good twenty years earlier.

- The same applies to weight. "A few pounds heavier" has become a very scary phrase in online gay interaction. You can say in your profile that you need to maybe drop a pound or two, and you can use a big, big font. But if the picture shows something more on the order of real paunch where your relatively fine waist should be, believe that it's the picture the men will trust, not the words.

- Try to appear natural, or as natural as anyone can seem while posing for the marketplace. Men who set up tripods to capture their hindquarters jutting out into the next room are trying too hard. Similarly, lying on your back and kicking out your leg like a Radio City Music Hall Rockette can seem just a little overdone. Besides, it's a flattering angle for very, very few.

REALITY CHECK

This is important, and daringly contrary to the demands of many of today's users: Take a single photo of all of your naked self that also clearly shows your face *only* if you are fully prepared to romp nude in the streets tomorrow, provided municipal laws so permit. It doesn't matter how adamantly very hot users—and it is only the very hot users who do it—insist upon a combined face and nude full-body shot. They fear risking their hotness on a fake, and want irrefutable proof that you are a worthy and whole package.

Too bad, boys. The apathy of the online world at large notwithstanding, the combined face-and-nude-body shot is simply asking for trouble.

- A photo of your face with a naked torso, however, is just fine. Everyone goes to the beach, right? Your genitalia can be shot separately. And don't let that sentence alarm you.

- The etiquette of sending pictures in response to requests via IMs is not very different from any other form of civility—that is, reciprocity—practiced in the real world. If you ask in an IM to see someone's photo, it is understood that you will be returning one of your own.

That's the inherent "law," unless you have made it known that you do not possess one and your new friend is okay with it.

If the picture you asked to see doesn't enchant you, you are nonetheless still obligated to e-mail your own. Remember, this is about basics. You, friend, initiated the exchange. It is juvenile and grossly unfair to back off because what you requested wasn't the stuff that dreams are made of. Which is why it's a very good idea to start by requesting a simple face-pic trade.

- Be it your digital camera or a friend's, erase, erase, erase. Then erase again.

- There's a whole lot of mockery these days directed at the nude self-image shot in the mirror. It's understandable; such photos tell the silly story of their taking, and we chuckle over the flash on the face and the many attempts we know to have been made to get as much hot body in the bathroom mirror reflection as possible. Pure amateur night, to be sure.

But you know what? They're okay. As long as the outcome shows what needs to be shown, the clumsy mode of the process should not be an issue. Besides, even at its most homespun and awkward, the self-taken picture is usually authentic. Picture scammers rarely try to pass off such amateur stuff as their own, and the odds are that the mirror shot was taken by that self and of that self.

- If you are of the breed who can achieve and maintain a state of tumescence (in lay terms, an erection) while simultaneously striking a pose in front of a mirror, obfuscating your face with either the camera itself or by standing on tiptoe, and sucking in whatever gut you may have, we salute you. For the rest of you, don't worry about it. Even in modern times, a little something should be left to the imagination.

The lack of an erection, in fact, is a handy conversation helper, as the recipient of the picture will then ask, in the awestruck tone of a little boy at the circus, how big it gets.

REALITY CHECK

It's hard to fathom why *anyone* would transmit a false picture to a prospective hookup when the deception will inevitably be unmasked at the meeting. The most common explanation going is that the culprit reasons that his soon-to-be partner will be so fired up he will not care.

You think? No? Of course you don't. Your state of lust may be nearly explosive, but you will nonetheless be suddenly flaccid when the sizzling hot, worked-out, and devilishly handsome fellow in the photograph appears at your door as, say, a pudgy senior citizen. There's no way around this, and it seems a pretty sure bet that only bragging from the practitioners of this ruse—bragging based on nothing but fantasy—keeps the ridiculous con going.

Adopt the charade of sending out a picture of someone else only if you are fully prepared to be sent packing three seconds after arriving. As, unfortunately, you will deserve.

TALES FROM THE WEB

A gentleman once sent out a picture of a porn star and claimed it as his own likeness. He believed that, as the porn actor in question was not as readily identifiable as, say, Brad Pitt, he could get away with it. What he could not know was that the recipient had always harbored an especial weakness for this particular stud. Moreover, the picture sent displayed the actor—partially, anyway—in a uniform he wore in the recipient's favorite film of his. All of which was mockingly pointed out to the sender in short order.

Nonetheless, the sender *insisted* it was himself. The recipient was disgusted, and ended the chat. The moral being that porn stars are stars because a lot of people have seen them. Don't imagine for a minute that the object of your interest hasn't viewed his share of dirty movies.

There's yet one other sidebar to this business. Not everyone who's sending out fake pictures—or even just relaying untrue descriptions of themselves—is actually out to delude. Some really believe themselves to be young when they are not, buff where they are not, and handsome when they are most assuredly not. It isn't that these men are deliberately misrepresenting themselves; it's that they maintain a self-image absolutely no one else can perceive.

Should you find yourself face to face with such a man, through misplaced trust or an especially excellent picture and/or presentation seeming, for all the world, like the real thing, back off. But back off gently. Invent whatever is necessary to end the date as quickly as possible. Don't confront with the idea of setting this not-fully-sane bastard right. You can't know his psyche, or how desperately tenuous his claim is to his fictive reality. It isn't any of your business, anyway. It's messy, marshy ground, and all you want to do is slip away as smoothly as possible.

This brings us to an almost metaphysical dimension of this game of photo swapping. How painfully accurate can you afford to be in a world where just about everyone is gilding the lily, and using gallons of gold paint to do it? Of course pictures partly remedy the problem. But there are real and hot men out there without pictures. You may not, for any of a number of legitimate reasons, feel comfortable sending a picture. All right. You may be decent-looking, yet you know that if you describe yourself modestly, you will come up empty. What to do? How much to stretch the truth of your not-at-all horrific looks?

On the whole, keep your stretching to an absolute minimum, if you must stretch at all. Or just don't stretch, period. Few of us are drop-dead handsome, and most of us are what is known as "nice-looking." Ironically, "nice-looking" is really just fine with the online gay community. It's when the nice-looking guy asserts that he is very, very, *very* good-looking that problems begin.

Last word on the picture scene: a lot of men are increasingly intolerant of, if not downright snide to, the user with no photograph to trade. They don't just move on; they insult and belittle the photoless chatter. "Get with it!" they bark. "It's the twenty-first century, for Christ's sake!" they bellow.

Ignore them. If you do not feel you can have a picture of yourself to ante up with, and you don't ask to see others under false pretenses, then your lack of an image is entirely your affair. Just tell it like it is. It is the safest policy because it is the *only* policy, for you and for any him out there. The pulls on your line may be fewer, but they will be more fruitful. Besides, as long as there's genuine confidence in the tone of the description you give, your appeal is exponentially enhanced. If X says he's not a bad-looking guy, X is going to generate some interest. But when X goes to great lengths to make it known that he is so hot, sidewalks bubble and churn under his feet, and then tells any and all interested parties that the dog ate his pictures . . . nope. No one possessed of really spectacular looks—and who enjoys the hell out of describing them—has no photo of himself to transmit online. As in real life, the gorgeous are fond of self-documentation.

IN ACTION

THE CHAT ROOM:
THE (VIRTUAL) COMPANY
YOU KEEP

We can talk to strangers
We are burning with the spark.
—*"We Close Our Eyes," Go West*

BOOKS OPEN? GOOD.

An online chat room is a block of web space designated as, and programmed to be, an instant message facility for more than two people. That is essentially it. Minor bells and whistles adorn most of them: private "sub" chats can be opened through the main one, customarily so that several of the men in the room can get especially nasty without the threat of a not-hot fellow joining in; some allow a mini posting of your photograph to accompany your name in the room's roster of visitors; and most let you format your text input—whatever it is you feel the need to say to the throng—any way you like, with color, font, italics, and all the emoticons you can slap on.

REALITY CHECK

If you're tempted to take advantage of the Crayola-like assortment of colors and fonts available for online communicating, pause first. Sure, you want to stand out. And if your prose subtly changes hue from blue to lilac, you *will* stand out. But not necessarily in the way you might want to. Think first about how you wish to be perceived, and remember that pretty, frilly letters usually indicate—fairly or not—a frilly person behind them.

There are, of course, many, many kinds of chat rooms provided by every ISP and dating site currently engaged in that arms race. All exist for one reason: to bring people together. There are so many because a lot of people are very, very eager to be brought together.

Within the universe of the romantic chat room are those catering to men honestly in search of women, men after men, women after women, and those guys and gals happy to spend some time with either gender. All these chats fall into that single, great, primary raison d'être of the Internet: people looking to find new people. And, of course, the focus here is the realm of the third category.

The first, however, merits an extra line. For the new, gay user with a liking for straight men may naively think the room named STR8DUDES4STR8DUDES is . . . well, straight.

It is not. It is Cubist. That is to say, straightness is in there somewhere, but it's lost in the overall picture. Make no mistake about it: The only *truly* straight rooms are, in fact, never identified as such. They are instead the chat rooms named for the city or state their guests inhabit, and bear no gender tag (such as "W4M" or "M4W"), whatsoever. Here, men, is where the honest-to-God heterosexual male searches for a female. Should you dip a toe into these waters, perhaps thinking the brass ring of real masculinity can be yours, be careful. These guys aren't suppressing much of anything, except maybe some serious issues with gay men who harass them in straight chats.

We narrow the field further, then.

Two basic types of chats exist for the gay man online. The first is location-specific. These are the CHICAGOM4M, ELPASOM4M, and PHILLYM4M rooms. The second type is a broad range, including but not limited to preferences in build (M4MMUSCLEBEARS), age (TWINKS4OLDER), generalized locale (STEAMROOMM4M), and—here we go, guys—straightness. The AOL chats purportedly closed off to all but straight, married men are seas of frantic gay messaging. They are often also the busiest rooms, requiring whole minutes of steady clicking before one patron exits and vacates a virtual chair.

So why are these rooms so popular if it's pretty quickly understood that gay sexuality runs just as rampant in them as in the gay-designated rooms? It's a mind-set thing. First, it is only to a room labeled as such that the rare genuinely bisexual or curious man—and they do exist, the necessary and many avowals to the contrary notwithstanding—will go. There is no other room he would *wish* to try, if he is what he is. Second, this very factor of occasional, real straight company encourages the men who may be gay but who have no time for the more effete of their ilk. In other words, more manly men.

Now, to business. You are set up with your screen name and profile. You have dutifully read the chapters regarding these virtual overcoats and are raring to go. You have an ISP, and you know where they keep their chats. You acknowledge that you are not quite prepared to jump into the chat room named after your own town and occupied by your neighbors. You decide to start easy and try a generic, non-location-specific gay chat. There is now nothing holding you back from entering this buzzing universe of gay interaction.

But you hold back. More than understandable. The degree of apprehension men feel before stepping into their first virtual chat is high and quite ordinary. You'd think it was a real room, wouldn't you? Actually, it *is* a real room, isn't it? No, it is not. It is a little real and a lot false. And this in itself should soothe your nerves, for the chat room experience plays out in such a way that you yourself have the power to make it as real as you'd like it to be, or as fake as the moment calls for.

Know this from the outset, and know it well: The gay chat is frequently looked to only for instant gratification purposes. In other words, porn. This is the "fake" aspect, the using of the room and the "real" men in it for the weaving of fantasies based on what they say about themselves, in profiles or in messages. For multitudes of users, the mere bandying of lewd IMs and the trading of nude photographs is more than enough. These exchanges are the virtual version of getting hot and bothered by the gorgeous guy at the adult bookstore. He's strutting and you'll never get within two feet of him, but the air is so charged with sexual tension, and the fantasies he elicits are so erotic, you don't need to. Now it's all at your desk, and you only need to get up to clean up.

There are those who resent playful intentions in an arena where they feel only direct, serious cruising should be taking place. They have no patience for "game players"; they decry the loiterers, the insincere. But they don't fully understand the turf they wish to protect. That is, they may as well picket Disneyland for employing actors, and not real cutthroats, in its presentation of Pirates of the Caribbean.

Because, ironically, the same, studly men who take exception to the chat-as-porn activity are largely responsible for it. Think for a moment about drawing twenty to thirty men into the same room. *In real life.* How many, do you suppose, would be amazingly hot? One, maybe, with a few not-bads in there? On a good day, perhaps. Meanwhile, the online novice enters *any* room marked for "hot gay/str8/curious" men, and his immediate impulse is to suck in his gut. Because here at least two-thirds of the inhabitants may as well be porn stars, based on their simmering profiles.

Gee, is this where all the exceptionally hot men are, then? Online, and consequently not available for a three-dimensional gathering? No. No, no. And this is the foundation of the looking-but-not-buying mentality that so enrages the serious cruiser: the excessively sexy—and not usually entirely accurate—self-portrayals. In a nutshell, quite a few of the men angry at insincere interplay within the chat feed the beast they dislike, through deliberately buffed-up, virtually pornographic, presentations of themselves.

Now, it might appear that deception and ruses are actually being promoted in chat room interaction. They are not. But they are there and they are not going anywhere. The virtual world has its own laws of physics, and they are—sensibly—based on the fact that lust-filled men will say anything to get the immediate gratification they require. Just as you don't go husband-searching in the video arcade, you aren't surrounded by the ethical codes of the Boy Scout in M4MNEEDSITNOW. A little invention is expected in these parts, guys.

But take heart. One good thing about the chat room is that the company is perpetually shifting. Yes, there are guys who plant themselves in chat room chairs and strap themselves in, seemingly for life. The Internet could come crashing down, but they ain't moving. But a lot of men have other things to do and, after about fifteen minutes or so, move on. The stalwarts aside, within a few hours hundreds of men will be in and out of the same room with space in it for only thirty to forty. As the number of visitors rises, so does that small percentage of the really hot. Hang around for a spell. That man you've dreamed of, either for an introductory chat or for a semifast, sexy hour at your place, is coming.

And *this* is wherein your ability to mark the line between bogus and genuine comes into play. Through IM contact, either received or initiated, sexual chemistry can be kindled. From there, and depending on how seriously you wish to pursue your correspondent, his mask or his authenticity will be determined. Both of you can maintain the contact at a pornographic, would-be-real-nice level. Both of you can then attend to business at your respective desks and go merrily on your individual offline ways. Perhaps one of you suspects the other sent a picture not of himself. Maybe neither fully trusts the vaunted masculinity of the other. But provided there is a healthy suspension of disbelief, no harm is done.

However, it may happen that the very sexy or romantically interesting guy with whom you are chatting noticed the city indicator in your screen name. It may be he messaged you, in fact, because he too lives there or is soon visiting that city, and you are someone he'd like to visit. Well, then. Enter reality. You may still string him along with vague assurances, taking advantage of the added dimension of reality in the scenario to enhance the business of the moment. Or you now have before you the option of arranging a likely hookup. In which case, you must engage in a lengthier dialogue, and one with some fact thrown in among the panting.

A tacit understanding will pass between you and your partner in the proposed liaison; the more serious each of you is, the more down to brass tacks each of you must get. Even if he is sincere, he may still not tell you that the picture he sent is two years old and he's gained a few pounds since. But—again, if he means business—he *will* tell you if the picture is eight years old and he's gone as bald as a melon in the intervening time. As you yourself will be forthright about your vitals.

Can either of you be trusted fully? No. For one thing, too many men online are happy to fill in the gaping holes within the *sort-of* attractive guy's profile, and not necessarily in an accurate way. A lot of chatters take the bare-bones profile strategy to an unhelpful, if not self-defeating, extreme. They list a few vitals but omit important preferences or facts, like the guy who describes himself as physically hot and something of a sex fiend, but who fails to mention a very committed partner in his life. Others simply take too general a path. They present an easygoing, appealing persona, but give absolutely no indication of the kind of man they seek. Which leaves the road wide open for the interested man to engage in some serious wish fulfillment, and to breezily edit the vague, appealing profile to conform to what he hopes it more fully reflects.

Then, subjective realities aside, we are all doomed to always envision our incipient partner as hotter than he is, even after we've seen the photo. It's a Hollywood thing, an American mythos that expects strangers to look utterly unblemished. When, according to the latest stats, we all have blemishes. Here too, optimism can be misapplied—and a kind of Photoshop within our brains—paving the way for real disappointment.

But if you both lay what you at least believe to be your cards on the table—and the sincerity level is something you must intuit through the contact—neither of you can go terribly wrong. What moves from fun and games to a set time and date is largely up to you. The user makes the chat what it is. The power is yours to wield or toss about a bit.

REALITY CHECK

No single thing, no one tool, is more valuable in the world of Internet communication than instinct. It will stir within you when you're engaged in that stimulating private chat, and it will tap you on your shoulder when the third, strangely annoying IM comes from the guy you had your doubts about. It will also get you sending a message to someone who seems to be average but who you sense is more attractive. Every time, in every instance, go with it. Your gut is your greatest ally here, always. Listen and obey.

Very good. You got your feet wet. You logged a little time in MENSEEKINGMUSCLE, and it was easy. You weren't raped, threatened, bashed, or laughed at. And no one identified who you really are—no one, you noticed, even wanted to go there. Of course not. They themselves would rather not be targeted as the brokers, carpenters, tax experts, or all-around family men they are, either. (Well, the *carpenter* might. But that's another story.)

So you are emboldened to step into a chat based on your location. Go for it. The give-and-take of sexual interplay will be the same. What will be obviously different is the level of expectation. In this territory you are supposed to be substantially more serious about your intentions. These are, after all, your neighbors. And most of them would very much like to get a little action next Thursday night.

Yes, this is pressure of a sort. Remember, though: *As long as you represent your actual intentions honestly*, you do not have to do a single thing you don't want to do. This may seem an unnecessary caution. Yet men often feel obligated to agree to potential hookups they have no desire to participate in. Many find themselves signing on the dotted line before they know it, when all they did was respond blandly to the persistent messages of an admirer.

Beware being excessively agreeable in this realm. It can create enemies, albeit harmless ones. (Note: Civility is another thing entirely. There is no reason to be rude or nasty to someone desiring you, simply because he is miles away from your notion of exciting. Sadly, though, just trying to be "nice" gets both of you in trouble.) The man hot on your heels will *not* perceive your friendly responses as a gentle rebuff. This is repeated later on because it is a crucial and often not comprehended fact. In such a situation, the wisest thing to do is say that you are sorry, but he is not your type. Then ignore any continued messages. You may have to. Again, this isn't about being cruel; the sad fact is, he will still, quite often, not get it.

In these location-based rooms, and from the get-go, *be firm*. Polite, but firm. And always err on the side of caution. The guy contacting you may have a smoldering profile, and you may be dumbstruck that he is right here in your town *and* all hot and bothered for you. Panting, you will agree to far too much based on what is still illusory. Then his picture arrives. It does not turn you on. You are even outraged that someone right here in White Plains, New York, lies as blatantly as the guys in STR8NHOT4STR8. But you got carried away, and now must either slink off into the night or attempt to convincingly throw some forgotten obstacles in the way of the meeting you were arranging. In which case, the best out is the slink-with-an-excuse: Say that your boyfriend/girlfriend/roommate just walked in and that you've got to be going. Later. (You may still find yourself Buddy Listed by this fraud; some guys never get it. But as one who's already seen what's behind this guy's curtain, you are freer than free to ignore and block.)

REALITY CHECK

Do not ever claim to live alone. As long as you wish your online behavior to be cordial, as long as you'd rather spare feelings than trample on them, make it clear that someone shares your life, even if nonromantically. Trust me, you will need that other person in your home. And should things actually work out with someone to whom you fibbed, the innocent lie will do no harm. Your new friend should, in fact, respect your screening process and be flattered that he made it through.

Thus, the world of the chat. The mechanics await you below. Among them are the strategies, defenses, postures, offenses, salutations, conversations, interactive techniques, and more than a few of the kinds of flesh-and-blood men who make it all possible, who make it sometimes infuriating, and who make it—at least often enough—worthwhile.

But first, a qualifier. It may seem, in reviewing the pages above, that the picture drawn for the reader is not exactly a jolly one. Rude demands for pictures, snubs from jock boys? Strange men, unwanted contact, undesirable exchanges? Why even enter the chat room, then? Why play at all?

Because we *do* play, men. And the online chat room is, all the many little miseries of it aside, a surpassingly convenient field. The bar or nightclub has one huge advantage over the chat, yes, and you know what it is. You are there. You are seeing both the loser and the guy you would kill to be with. Deception may still run rampant, but no one there is going to lie about what he looks like, how masculine he is, and how attractive he is to you. Not very successfully, anyway.

But the online chat has advantages found in no other venue. The curious man who would not dare walk into the bar will try the chat, and perhaps try more from it. Most chats are open 24/7, too. And as in life, sometimes the most exciting men can be found at the oddest hours. In a sense, the old-fashioned farmer's work ethic applies to gay chats; the very early morning hours are the most fruitful. Not too shocking, because men are men, and it's no secret what state they're in upon awakening.

Now think of all the bar and club hours you yourself have logged. How much frustration, how many wasted nights, how many insipid conversations have you endured? Quite a lot. Certainly more than what was, afterward, worth it. Gay bars, gay chats, bookstores, bathrooms, online message boards, and offline wall graffiti: It's all one vast arena, with their own peculiar hindrances and assets. And sometimes you want to play from—as the TV ads used to say—the comfort of your own home. In—as the TV ads rarely said—your boxer shorts.

So welcome to the chat room, friend. This is where, despite everything the media likes to promulgate, the heart and soul of online life lies. (And lies, and lies, but that's in later chapters.)

The last word on the subject is a list of wisdom, bits of advice, and reiterations of points that need to be stressed. Take hold of your yellow highlighter, and read on.

• When you have lived in various cities, you begin to observe a refreshing parallel to real life within the online world. That is, all the hot guys are in other cities. The ass, so to speak, is always greener in the other guy's yard.

• Upon entering any of the many dozens of sex-related chat rooms for the first time, you notice that almost half of the dialogue screens are utterly blank. But don't hurry away. You have, in fact, found a good one. The dearth of common dialogue means that the thirty-odd specimens of steaming sexiness in the room are targeting one another individually. This is the cyber equivalent to the men who take a place at the bar and quietly hang out, addressing no one publicly but advertising their willingness to be addressed. And in this sort of musical chairs, you have a better chance of winding up on a hot guy's virtual lap.

• "MM" stands for "married man." A great many married men occupy chat rooms devoted to the pursuit of gay sex. From this you might presume that an equal number of married women are similarly busy in online galleries geared for lesbians. They are not. They are drinking or shopping. And you really can't blame them.

- Just as men have traditionally sought to attract females by the seemingly perverse bait of pretending to be married, so too do they fib when fishing for dudes. Why? Because in quite a few gay psyches, a married man is more desirable than a homosexual man. If men were grails, the married man would be the holy one, at least to a substantial gay demographic. In lustful online communication, expect no greater degree of veracity in this regard than you can reasonably look for elsewhere. Meaning, none.

- There is a horizontal bar below the chat room dialogue box. It is for sending messages to all in the room, for—*ahem*—conversation. Do not use it. There is little point, unless joining in on a series of bitchy remarks about who is going to what bar later, and which drag queen at said bar is most unaccomplished constitutes your idea of a stimulating exchange.

- Besides these armchair quarterback analyses of happy hours and female impersonation, the dialogue box is customarily punctuated by blatant demands for satisfaction. Let's just say that these cries of need are best ignored. Hunger lies within the text of the instant message, as sent to a specific user; the shout for immediate gratification posted for all to see is outright desperation.

- The above notwithstanding, one reason exists for quickly scanning the dialogue box: Often within those demands of satisfaction are the statistics of interesting guys whose profile you've not yet examined. Maybe you felt no strong pull to read Bill343's online bio after seeing his rather nondescript name in the visitors list. But when Bill posts for all to see that he is twenty-five, has arms the size of tree trunks, a girlfriend out of town, and pictures to trade, you may think again.

• Occasionally a nonparticipating attendee in a room will be referred to by someone as cluttering up the dialogue box with emoticons and sighs over that man's profile photograph. If you are that attendee, do not address the comment, whatever it may be. It only takes one wrong step to plunge into a well.

• About that Buddy List, first offered up by the obliging AOL and since then duplicated in chats everywhere: *Use it sparingly.* By the most conservative estimation, eight out of ten online men couldn't tell you who a fraction of the guys on their Buddy List are, when they added them, and why they felt the impetus to, whenever the hell it was.

Oh, but they know why, of course. It was nothing but the heat of the moment and the fever pitch of that chat. At that moment they are completely sure that they have stumbled onto the hottest guy in cyberspace. Three days later it's a dim, cleaned-up memory, and the saved name itself has lost all meaning. Abusing your Buddy List and stacking it with such fleeting scene-players isn't the worst thing you can do, and the list is easily pared down with a few clicks of the delete button. But in the realm of cruising or looking for serious affection, it can be an annoying, self-defeating burden. Go easy with it.

• Feast days. These are the hours in which you are unaccountably the hottest thing since before Mark Wahlberg put his pants on and became a movie star. IM after IM flies at you. Names concocted with dizzying eroticism are asking you what you are into. And you think, *Jesus Christ, where were all these guys yesterday? What is it about me today that has drawn this horde of buffness to me?*

Nothing. Except maybe that, as in life, you are most sought after when you care little about being attractive. For that is when the feast days occur. Yes, this is inexplicable. How can your nonchalance regarding popularity possibly be perceived through machines spread out all over the world? Yet this is precisely what happens. We are waiting for the mind that can properly account for this invisible variation of a syndrome seemingly dependent upon being visible. Whatever the reasoning, though, don't allow yourself to become more than temporarily complacent. Because as surely as night follows day, there will be . . .

• Famine. You've just left the gym. You feel large. You are horny. You go online, your studly confidence feeding into the keyboard. No one gives you the time of day. Damn,

damn, damn. It seems that the same eerie mechanism that telegraphs your desirable give-or-take attitude on feast days has a flip side to it. Do not dwell on any of this. Ride it out. Tides come in and tides go out, and everything is a matter of time.

• It happens, sad to say, that quite often the chat room you most wanted to enter—the one built around the lusty bucks in your own city—is the most dull. Not unexpectedly, you see the same names populating it day after day. You scroll and scroll, only to read the same awful jokes, the same assessments of last night's TV fare, and the same in-house rivalries and alliances. You despair of ever connecting with anyone hot and exciting within its cyber walls. This is understandable. But as overused as the metaphor of fishing is to online cruising, it is useful. Fishing involves hours of fruitless waiting, and sometimes whole days pass with only catches barely larger than the dimensions of the bait. Yet fishing teaches patience better than any other recreation devised by man. One hangs in and the line is pulled, even by some serious aquatic flesh. Ask any fisherman.

So as pointless and frustrating as keeping yourself listed in the room often is, keep visiting, at least from time to time. Only in this manner—and by never participating in the vapid chat taking place in the room's dialogue box— can you be noticed by the most prized catches of all: the hot businessman visting town, the amazing trainer from the gym, the confused and lovably clumsy jock. These are the sailfish of chat room life, and your only hope to get them hanging above your mantel is through being visible for them.

THE USUAL SUSPECTS: CHAT ROOM REGULARS

WHEN A NEWCOMER TO THE GAY ONLINE SCENE FIRST peruses the lists of names in the various chat rooms open to him, he usually gets a little giddy, a little lightheaded. He doesn't feel like he's merely found a new portal to the world of men; he feels like he's discovered a whole new species. He reads the profiles, he looks at the pictures posted, he gets hit with masculine, confident IM after IM. And he thinks that he really should have gone online long ago. Clearly, *this* is where all the attractive, fascinating men have gone to.

Then he begins making contacts. Some lengthy IM dialogues, some picture trades, some tentative get-togethers planned and carried out. And then the walls, as it were, come a-tumbling down. Weeks after that first, dizzy entry into gay cyber interaction, he signs on again and hears himself muttering, "Damn. Same old tired gang." Why, it's almost like he never found a new world of men at all.

It gets better. Time passes and our novice is now a veteran. He is planning a move to a new town, so he begins checking out the guys who hang in the chat rooms there. And extraordinarily, our user once more believes in that mystical place he's already been to and found unsettlingly like the world outside his door. He spies fresh names and fresh profiles, and he is captivated all over again. *So* that's *what was wrong*, he thinks. *This is where the men I want are.* He packs, he moves, he unloads the truck, he goes online. Two weeks later he commences doing precisely what he did back at the old homestead: alternately remaining hidden outside the rooms yet keeping an eye peeled for anything decent, or jumping in and praying that there's a soccer players' convention in town for the weekend.

Types. Too well-known types, and too familiar kinds of men: they occupy the cubicles next to us at the office, they occupy the stools beside us at the club, and they're every bit as present in virtual gay space. This is the way things are. And if by any chance you're harboring that sweet notion that another town is home to a different and better breed, remember *The Wizard of Oz* and one of its unfair and far too true lessons: If it isn't in your own backyard, it wasn't ever anywhere.

However, bustling metropolis or one-horse village, certain men can be counted on to fill the chat room landscape. So let's take a look at the various sorts of chat room guys you're either

REALITY CHECK

Big cities have a lot more guys than small cities. Understood. Also, big-city life tends to encourage men to make the most of themselves; more of them work out, more of them keep themselves well-groomed, and most of them try to look as sharp as possible because they're competing in a fast-paced market, and for everything that market has to offer.

So it's easy to figure that your chances of finding a terrific guy are better when you venture into the cities. Well, yes. But only as long as you go in knowing that the accessibility of these guys is commensurate with their greater attractions. The hot New Yorker may be looking for company, just as you are. But he's a tougher customer than the hot guy from Iowa. His awareness of his appeal is part and parcel of his armor for the life he leads, and his own standards, barricades, and everything else are just that much more difficult to surmount.

going to run into or have already run from. Maybe you won't want to play in these arenas much. But it never hurts to know who the other players are, what they do, and how they do it.

The Queen Bee is the one who has taken it upon himself to rule the room, and usually with an iron fist. This pitiable individual is clearly in desperate need of esteem, and he squeezes it out of strangers who are too bored to dethrone him.

He is easily identified, for he will be in the room almost all the time. He will also have a cute and/or clever name; it will never be straightforward or short, because he is too complex a soul for brevity. And that name will flash on the dialogue screen with a frequency to shame a strobe light.

There are variations within this type. Most are overtly and proudly gay, yet others occupy supposedly straight rooms and play to a nauseating level a sort of good-guy, laid-back game. That is, they believe every comment of theirs a definitive statement on whatever foolishness is being spewed and scrolled on the dialogue screen. Others reign through a Wal-Mart–like role of greeter. They are everyone's friend. They are a pain in the ass because one doesn't always want one's dirty name thrown into the dialogue screen in big blue letters and with five exclamation points after it.

Arranging an actual hookup with the Queen Bee—should there be hotness somewhere beneath the robes—is supremely doable. The overtly gay specimen is, in fact, the most accessible of all the usual suspects. All you need do is IM as a supplicant: Ask him about the room, bow to his expertise, laugh at his jokes, and present yourself as desirable along the way. Forgive the crassness, but if you bullshit, he will come. And he will most definitely be talking about you later, and you know where.

THE WHIIIIIINER

This specimen may be the most common in gay chats. He is known all too well to many of the others present. His calling card is an endless slipping in of laments about his lack of a partner, peppered with avowals about his willingness to do anything to get him one and what he thinks are funny remarks about his solitary situation. He would never believe himself to be a Whiiiiiiner. In his mind, his wit obviates his self-pity.

His screen name is artistic and is sometimes phrased as a question. His profile is long and tiresome and ends in a lengthy essay on how few real people there are out there and how weary he is of being fooled by the less than real. (Note: The tenacity of the Whiiiiiiner is nothing to sneeze at, for he welcomes the God (see p. 90) into the room with many an exclamation point. And when he doesn't receive a response, he will doubtless besiege the mythical bastard with a series of importuning IMs.)

It doesn't matter how hot the Whiiiiiiner seems to be (and hotness is typically not the biggest gun in his arsenal). Steer clear, friends. The Whiiiiiiner is less a man and more a sack bursting full of needs. It's not that he can't be hooked up with; it's more that you won't ever get away with merely a hookup. You will have a . . . friend for life.

THE YAWNER

Cousin to the Whiiiiiiner, the Yawner is perhaps the second most commonly found chat room visitor. For he is the one who enters the albeit pointless dialogue only to remark upon how boring it is, and how bored he is, and how boring the day and everything in it is. He sings this song with gusto to rival Liza Minnelli's, and he sings it long.

The Yawner is a strange beast; clearly too bright for those surrounding him, he is nonetheless incapable of grasping the fact that his unendurable boredom is not likely to be alleviated by his spending hours bemoaning it.

In his defense, the Yawner occasionally tries to get things moving. He does this by sporadically and nastily asking the whole room what, exactly, their problem is.

THE SNIPER

This is the guy—often someone either a little too excessively devoted to his religion, or harboring serious sexuality issues— who jumps into gay rooms to bash. He will frequently ask what those freaks are doing in there. He then furiously asks why said freaks don't prefer the anatomical attractions of females. Feel for the Sniper, for these are questions that trouble him deeply.

He is known by his execrable spelling and grammar, and his queries are often in multicolored fonts. For considerable amounts of time, he sticks around the very rooms that so disgust him. Well, research is research.

THE HUSTLER

Hats off to the modern entrepreneur! Male escorts have long since discovered the rich fields of the chat room, and I salute their industry.

Often the Hustler sensibly and politely incorporates his vocation within his screen name with a dollar sign woven into it, as in "LAE$cort" or "MU$CStd4U." Others are more cagey. Their names will entice you to examine their profiles; once in, you will learn the score, if not the price. My personal favorites are the career boys, the ones who slyly refer to wanting a "generous" friend. Who says the age of the bimbo chorus girl is gone?

THE GHOST

This is the creature who takes care to devise a profile so enticing that thousands of desks tilt over thousands of male users, who sets himself up in the corner of the chat room, and who won't reciprocate contact. From anyone.

His name is the most dependable giveaway. It will be amazing, something by rights attached only to a pornographic superhero. His profile will be so masculine, it will stink of perspiration. And he occupies the room 24/7. Or, at least, his name does. The Ghost is the online and killer-sexy counterpart to the lost city of Atlantis: It's supposed to be fantastic, but odds are no one's actually going there anytime soon.

This is the verbose, active relation of the Ghost. This individual boasts the same extraordinary physical dimensions and the same unassailable divinity as as his ephemeral namesake. He is one tough customer also, as he has the right to be. His profile so plainly avers that he is not looking, so definitively states that he gets all he wants whenever he wants it and certainly doesn't need to get any from you, and so emphatically reinforces that he is as studly as he says he is, that you might begin to wonder how this specimen survives breathing the same air as lesser fry like your own poor self.

What turns the God on is—surprise!—attention. He is a good-natured son of a gun within the room dialogue, glad to joke around with the subspecies just as long as the occasional homage is made. In so doing, he unfortunately encourages mad daring; a bold but intrinsically unworthy soul may venture to scale the barbed wire the God has woven about his magnificence. Swatting such impertinence away is the price the God must pay for being so darn friendly. He will, in fact, sometimes refer to the unfairness of this arrangement, that he must be troubled when he has so graciously filled the room with perfection. It makes the God sad. You should be sad for him too.

"God," incidentally, is by no means meant sarcastically here. Only someone with divine abilities could actively occupy a chat room for the better part of each day and still maintain so sensational a body.

Now, it is possible to hook up with the God. But it ain't

easy. It is, rather, a more drawn-out business than anything you will engage in offline. It calls for sustained, nonintrusive persistence, and I mean *persistence*. It will take literally months of IMs. And never once in your genial approaches can you betray that you want him. What you are doing is slowly allowing him to see that you don't want him, and this is the only lure that works with such a fantastic fish.

Two warnings: After all your time and effort, he will be disappointing. That is a sad given. Also, gauge your commitment to this goal in regard to the prize. You can spend endless weeks, even a full year, in drawing him to you, or you could read *War and Peace*. Trust me, go for the Tolstoy.

THE PSYCHO

Don't be afraid—he can't get at you through the screen.

This is a very peculiar creature indeed. The Psycho sees your name in the chat room and initiates contact in an IM. Hence it would seem he is interested in you. Maybe he is. But the Psycho doesn't take the time-honored course of friendliness to indicate this. Instead, he is oddly and instantly hostile. He sneaks bitchy little remarks in between ordinary comments. You can't possibly reply quickly enough to satisfy him, which he then uses as proof of your insincerity. And when you decide that this is at best an unnecessary chat and ignore him, the Psycho will often go full tilt and blatantly, hysterically insult you, the very person he wanted to contact.

How can we explain the chat room Psycho? In real life he is the annoying son of a bitch who has no notion that his behavior is odious. He thinks he's funny. He is the beast with the rationale of jabbing-as-courtship. May he one day find the person to whom this is endearing.

THE BRUISER

Related to and sometimes mistaken for the Sniper or the Psycho, the Bruiser lives for trouble. You'll know him by, if nothing else, the trail that follows him in the chat room—an endless stream of requests that he get the hell out of there. He will, too, as soon as a room moderator throws him out or he gets bored with the prey currently at hand.

Until then he will jab at everything and everyone. No one is safe. He goes after an individual and abuses him on the dialogue screen because . . . well, because he noticed him, or he goes off on a rampage against the whole collective. None of it will be founded on anything at all, and the more he is encouraged to exit, the more he snarls and kicks. The visual image of the Bruiser is the worst school bully you can conjure, rocketed into space and blindly flailing in the vast emptiness.

These are the men in the rooms, make no mistake about it. They're the guys who IM you, scan your profile and address you in the dialogue screen, e-mail you with unasked-for pictures of themselves, or utterly ignore you.

But they are, luckily, merely a percentage of the men checking in. The other ones, the ones you are out to meet, will be stopping by too. These are the virtual versions of the sexy guys walking past on the street, the ones you'd like to wave and greet. And thanks to the friendly, accommodating instant message feature, you can.

INSTANT MESSAGING:
THINKING INSIDE THE BOX

THE CHAT ROOM IS THE MEDIUM; THE INSTANT MESSAGE is the . . . well, message.

With millions upon millions of men online every day, the IM is the tool that allows you to get the attention of just one, to privately "whisper" in his ear. Almost every form of chat you will come in contact with permits individual messaging. The AOL version is true to its famously user-friendly agenda; click on the name you like, then click on "Instant Message." A rectangular box will pop up in the upper left corner of your screen, and your cursor will be obligingly poised at the ready for you to say the hello you want to say. Other providers' messaging differs in how you connect directly to another chat guest—some IM boxes are front and center, some make cute little noises, some keep the messaged person's photo in your view, etc.—but the mechanics are basically the same. The individual connection is always, always made easy. If you think *you* want to score, the chat host seemingly wants you to score more than you do.

Is the instant message feature valuable? No. It is *essential*. It is what you are in the chat room for, really. Yes, lots of gay men do delight in the communal conversations of the room's main screen. More do not. They do not with a vengeance. When these men go online under their erotic screen names, they do not do so to waste their time and energy contributing bitchy phrases about Brad Pitt, the weather, or who was hot last Saturday night at the neighborhood pub. They are online to get the job done, by hookup or otherwise. For this, the IM is what users need, it allows direct, one-on-one contact.

Think of the IM box as the street corner of online life. People bump into one another there, shake hands, walk past without a second look, and sometimes—usually late in the evening—lower their standards. It is the portal not to the people, but to the person. It is the howdy-do you extend to the businessman on the prowl, the A&F boy, the discreet traveler lodging at the local Holiday Inn.

What goes wrong with most IMs is what usually can't go amiss in real life exchanges. In real life, the guy after the other guy's attention sees and adapts to the object's availability. He has to because it's all right there in front of him, whether it be the cell phone in his hand or the casual conversation he's engaged in with someone else who's with him. Online, the man initiating the contact is blithely assuming his object is not otherwise engaged, or is at that moment as receptive to getting a message as the initiator is eager to send it. This seems a fairly small obstacle. It is not. It is huge.

The *only* thing you can be sure of about the guy you're messaging is that he is somehow connected to the Internet just then. If he's actively involved in chatting, then he's definitely giving it some of his attention. But there's still a world of other factors and possibilities to consider, even within this narrowed view.

Your frame of mind while at your computer is as subject to variations of mood as it is anywhere else. You sit down at your computer, log in, and head for the nearest, best gay chat room. JOEnPhoenix has an interesting profile, so you IM JOEnPhoenix. No response. You wait a little bit and decide to give Joe another go. Nothing pushy, just a "You there, buddy?" As you wait, you scroll up to scan the room dialogue. Yes, there he is; he tossed in a comment or two only a few minutes earlier. Seems like a nice guy, too. But you don't want to press it. So you forget about Joe, thinking he has read your profile and written you off as bad news. You move on, but you're a little peeved at this jerk, JOEnPhoenix.

You were right the first time, though. Joe's a pretty cool guy. What you can't know is that in the time since he dropped that last genial remark in the room dialogue, Joe was totally rebuffed by someone he thought was a living god. Two minutes before that, a porn site he stumbled onto crashed his computer and he had to reboot. And just as you were typing in your second quick IM, his roommate knocked on his door, Joe said he was busy, and Joe could then hear the roommate snickering in the arrogant conclusion that Joe was doing just what he had thought Joe was doing. Gandhi would snap under these circumstances, and you got off easy by merely being ignored.

You yourself did nothing wrong at all. Your timing was off, is all. But what's important here is that you saw Joe as an inconsiderate jerk because you *assumed* he was at his desk and as free as you were. Easy to do. Every minute, men message guys who have been more than eager to chat with them on other occasions, only to be left staring at a blank space where the reply should be. Too often they fire another inquiry at the strangely silent chatters. Far too often they add sexual content to the second or third IM to *really* get their attention. And what these persistent IMers get back is usually a terse request to leave them alone, because they are not by themselves just then.

Are these men lying? Have they entered chat rooms only to tease and irritate? Hardly. It's a fair supposition that they logged in to the chat for the exact reasons you did. A man's presence in a gay chat is the red flag flipped up on his virtual mailbox, and he knows it. But noncyber, in-the-real-life-room interference still exists. You'll find, too, that fresh contact may come later from the one who put you off, and his reasons are often valid. But it doesn't matter; at that moment, the sender isn't welcome. End of story. Move on.

JACK MAURO

Remember, we are all online in the dark. The best thing you can bear in mind when you consider sending an IM to a stranger is what you know quite well: You have *no idea* what else this individual is up to right then. You can make an educated guess, yes. But in online cruising there are hundreds of other possibilities, not the least of which is that your dream man may be nearing a crescendo of a very hot exchange with someone else. Or he may be busy juggling several IM conversations before your little box pops up on his screen.

In real life—at a bar, say—you would see from across the room how occupied that guy you like is. And odds are, you wouldn't push his other would-be suitors out of the way with your bare hands, because that sort of determination tends to turn people off. Here you're seeing nothing. So that friendly, neutral shout is the best you can do. The rest is up to him.

All the necessary cautions aside, you are entitled to IM him. Send a message, say hello, slap that gorgeous fellow on the back with a few words. The instant message is the tool kept on the top of the box, and for good reason. Just don't take too much of any of it personally. These are strangers you're dealing with, after all. Many are fakes and some are real, and of these, a few you find attractive and/or are attracted to you.

Keep it simple, keep it civil. And above all, don't lose sight of the fact that your online senses are limited. Remember the now classic cartoon of the canine at a keyboard, gleefully saying, "Online, no one knows you're a dog"? You need to remember also that online, phones still ring, moods change, and unwelcome roommates knock. For everyone.

DOS, DON'TS, AND MORE DON'TS

Evil communications corrupt good manners.
—1 Corinthians 15:33

TO CATALOG EVEN THE MOST BASIC RULES AND STRATEGIES of instant messaging is inherently not possible. As stated earlier, what we're talking about here is human interaction. It may take place on a screen, but all the millions of variables, all the quirks and etiquettes, and all the potential responses and dialogues within any couple's verbal intercourse nonetheless come into play. Scholars have invested years and written volumes on the subject as it is practiced in real, non-Internet life alone.

However, there *are* aspects to this interplay that belong uniquely to the IM. Let's have a look at the most prominent.

THE APPROACH

It is a curious thing, the differences one sees in IM approaches. There are those men who, upon spotting a name and finding it stimulating, hurl a one-word interrogatory: "Stats" or "Looking" or "Top." (These pursuers don't actually add a question mark to their staccato demands, but that's a shorthand talked about later.) Then there are those just as aroused but seemingly are from a more genteel world. They will go through the motions, like a society hostess pouring tea, of grammatically correct chitchat: "How's it going?" and "Hey, buddy. How are you doing?" Both parties on either side of the IM know full well what the object is, of course. Yet the latter IMer takes his hat off first. This is an excellent practice; we need to hold on to all the fundamental courtesy left on the Internet that we can.

TO IGNORE OR NOT TO IGNORE, THAT IS THE QUESTION

This is a pickle.

You probably never meant to ignore anyone, or you're new to the instant message game and you just can't see yourself doing it. How much time does it take, after all, to send a brief reply to someone, especially someone nice enough to be interested in you? And how much better a cyberworld would it be if everyone just practiced this minimal courtesy?

This is an admirable attitude, and you should maintain it *whenever possible*. Unfortunately, it just isn't always possible; sometimes you actually have to be ruthless. Because a lot of the "interest" you generate will not be the kind you want, and no amount of gentle, dissuading messaging you do will make it go away.

Think about a real-life encounter of a similar nature: You're at a party, you're minding your own business, and suddenly someone you're uninterested in approaches. You are polite, but in no way encouraging. In fact, your body language, tone, and curt replies pretty definitively spell out that you'd rather be left alone. But he isn't budging. So you pretend to spot a dear old friend across the room, ask to be excused, and walk the hell away as fast as you can without breaking into a run.

It's much the same in these cyber waters. Nowhere does the old saw about being cruel to be kind apply more than in IM intercourse. The cruiser you want nothing to do with, and to whom you are merely gracious, will *not* perceive your response as perfunctory politeness. He will seize upon your "interest" as a godsend. This in turn launches you into a weary dance of ever more direct rebuffs until the point is made.

REALITY CHECK

There is little room for subtlety online. Nuance, sarcasm, and irony, so effective in face-to-face mating scenarios, are almost impossible to convey in IM boxes. Here the printed word is everything. This makes for a hard world, but it can be a more efficient one too.

It did not occur to you, but the undesirable citizen you were foolish enough to be nice to took advantage of the Buddy List option. You were open to him. You didn't ignore him, as so many other guys do, so in his eyes you both deserve and want his attention whenever you go online. In other words, you've been earmarked as a special friend by someone you never want to see on your screen again.

A day passes. You log on and suddenly he's there, slapping you with an IM greeting. You can't even jump in for a fast e-mail check without his finding you. Damn. Nice guys *do* finish last, it seems.

What to do? Simple. With one hand, you reply in a pleasant, easygoing way. With the other, you go into your preferences in your toolbar, access the privacy section, and enter the pest as someone to be blocked. Then IM him that the bathwater is overflowing and you have to go. Voilà! You are free, and with no direct attack on the hapless soul's feelings.

JILTED AT THE KEYBOARD

The plain fact is that online and driven by desire, your lust is running the show. When a very attractive user profile sparks the flame, you want badly to get that fellow's attention in an IM. So you send the message. Nothing comes back. You wait. You send another leading phrase, equally cool. You are still the only one writing in the box. You wait even longer this time. Again no one's home.

Do you keep trying? Sadly, you often do, even though you know full well that the first message was the best you could do.

Don't do this. If your first IM gathers dust, then that is what it does. He most likely won't respond if he hasn't within a minute or two, and you will most assuredly not increase your chances of making contact by howling at his door. Yes, maybe he did step away from his computer for a moment. He might very well come back with that fresh cup of coffee and be delighted to see that first greeting of yours. But if he returns to see a string of increasingly desperate/pleading/angry questions waiting on his screen, there's a good chance your name's going to join his "blocked" roster.

As gay chat issues go, this is one large and very bitter pill to swallow. But rules are rules. When the amazing gentleman you attempt to draw into conversation does not respond, do not scramble for possible face-saving rationales. Do not persist in messaging him in the fantasy that he has been called away from his computer. Do not court further rejection by assaulting him with more boxes. Better men have managed to get this medicine down. Do likewise, gentlemen. Take it for what it is: rejection. And move on.

FEAST DAYS

It's a happy time when you log on, enter a chat room, and are slammed with IM after IM. You're suddenly the most popular guy in the world, and it can be an exhilarating boost to the ego. It can also be a sea of frustration. Someone eminently desirable messages you, and you begin to reply, only to see your cool encouragement partially typed into a new box slapped over the good one, and then another fresh box slapped over that one. When multiple IMs start rolling in, it is dizzying. It's like a crazy poker game, with no time allowed for more than the briefest glance at your hand.

Keep your cool. Think priority management. Take the moment needed to assess each correspondent. It is easy not to; it is easier to throw up a fast "hey, man" than to scan that person's profile. But take that little bit of time anyway. It will save you in the long run—the long run being those few minutes when all this activity is coming to a close and you want to emerge from it with the best of all contacts.

REALITY CHECK

Online communication has been likened to chess. It is not remotely like chess. Chess is best played when long thought goes into each move. Online, speed is paramount. The better metaphor is the OK Corral. You draw quick in these parts, or you're history. And when you're the golden boy and lots of hot men are sending you IMs, it's a good idea not to stay too long in the chat where it all started. You've got plenty to keep you busy for the time being.

Let's not forget Mr. Short-Term Memory. He is out there, and he has many guises. He is the fellow who IMs you as a stranger only days after you shared a prolonged IM conversation. Normally, this is rectified quickly, and a photo resend usually does the trick. He can be forgiven, under the circumstances. In a world bursting with thousands of scrambled versions of what is essentially the same name, anything like decent recall takes on the aura of a mutant talent.

When this happens, be kind. Don't get all huffy that you weren't properly remembered. Because you too will be, now and then, Mr. Short-Term Memory. There are just too many connections for it not to happen. There are also more than a few men who operate under several screen names and who will expect you to miraculously know who they are under each different label.

And when it's your own memory lapse at play? How do you react when reminded that your new correspondent is, in fact, an acquaintance from a long private chat you had last Thursday? Not a problem. Since *you* conducted yourself decently in that first conversation—as *you* always do—your friend has no reason to exact revenge. He may be a little hurt, yes. But provided this is someone you'd like to keep in contact with, all you need do is a verbal smack to the head and roll of the eyes, and say you're sorry. If he's especially worth welcoming back, say something to the effect of how dumbfounded you are that you could forget such a babe. Flirting—at a party, in a club, or through a keyboard—it's gold.

One more plus in this scenario: If the guy is amazingly hot and you failed to recognize him on the second go-round, *you* become in his eyes all the more desirable.

LISTENING TO YOUR "SIX PACK"

There's a singular aspect to IMs, which is that there are times when, despite the ordinary quality of the words in the box flashing before you, you find yourself reacting with antipathy. Something about that phrasing you've seen a million times before is off-putting. You have no reason to dislike the sender— he may actually have an especially enticing profile—but you do dislike it. Based on nothing at all, you do.

Go with it. Your instincts are kicking in, and only a fool sets them aside. One day science will explain just how the transference of binary code on a screen can intrinsically convey the essence of the sender. Till then, however, obey that hunch and snub the bastard.

THE LANGUAGE

If anything is to reshape the written word as it is used today, it will not be the news media. It will not be Hollywood, Nashville, or Fitty Cent. It will be the notorious time constraints of the instant message.

To a newcomer to the scene, it's a mess. He's expecting to see sentences laid out in English; what he is confronted with instead is a bizarre Esperanto comprising primarily hieroglyphics. There are probably fresh dictionaries out there right now, aimed at deciphering this new language, and they're probably out-of-date before the ink is dry. There are just too many abbreviations and symbols, the list grows daily, and there can't be much need to educate people that "u" is meant to stand in for "you." Suffice it to say what you already know: The IM requires a kind of lay stenography, a shorthand dictated by the pressure of time.

How far you are willing to compromise is entirely up to you. Your mood of the moment often calls the shots, as does the style of the person messaging you first. If you see "sup" flash at you, feel as free as a bird to be as monosyllabically drab as you like. Conversely, a carefully typed out "Hey, how are you?"—and this is Miltonic poetry in this neck of the woods—might elicit a more proper "Good, and you?"

All told, it is easier to initially like the fellow who can form a sentence. Yet nothing really changes, does it? Be it the Wild West of the 1800s or the zippy era of the Pentium PC, the schoolteacher, sadly, is never as hot as the illiterate gunslinger.

ONLINE MORALITY AND THE INFAMOUS "LTR"

Some blinders-wearing chaps insist in their profiles that they are not, and they mean *not*, interested in hooking up. Some have happy long term relationships (LTRs); some refuse to debase the value of their prospective LTR appeal by sleeping around. Strangely, though, these very champions of keeping the knees together will be the ones to IM you. They liked your profile. You sound hot and interesting.

How to react? And why waste the time, anyway, since based on the guy's profile vow of chastity, nobody's pants will be descending?

Respond if the profile points to a genuinely hot man. Ignore the LTR stuff, particularly when his opening remark to you is flirty or just plain sexual. Don't even refer to it, to remind your correspondent of his once-nobler aspirations. Kafka said letter writing is intercourse with ghosts, implying that the time passed between the sending and the reading often means your letter is reaching something of a different person from the one you put pen to paper for.

To do Franz further justice, it's worth noting that we frequently address who we wish that person to be, rather than who he is. (What existentialist good times Kafka could have had with online life! But that's speculation for another day.) The man who described himself as unwilling to hook up was in one frame of mind when he wrote that profile, as was the man who was new to online cruising and, just then, pleased with his LTR. And no single thing on the planet vanishes as quickly as a man's better nature once he starts feeling frisky. A massive storm cloud can blot the sun over vast acreage in a heartbeat—it is not as fast. When the man with the hands-off profile contacts you, rest assured, he wants hands. Whether or not to give them is, of course, your call.

Profiles stored with any ISP may be updated hourly. It matters little. Most of us don't update. Most of us, in fact, can't remember what the hell we put in ours. The guy who added his age to his profile back in 2003 didn't *intend* in a diabolically farsighted way to lie to the men of 2007; he just forgot about it and is still forgetting about it as the years roll on. Not updating the profile is the Internet version of the stereotypical guy's refusal to get up and change the channel when the dog has run off with the remote. It's ridiculously easy to do. But he'd rather not.

So it becomes less mysterious, then, when the guy with the glorious relationship described in his profile puts a cyber hand on your online leg. Maybe the relationship cooled since the writing. Maybe it evolved into a more open arrangement. Maybe the other guy skipped town. The profile, in today's world, is always the last to know.

I HEAR MUSIC . . .

In order to enhance the experience of communicating, many online chat rooms enable their subscribers to add a sound, a short bar of music, or a pain-inducing sound effect to their online entrances and exits. So would a misguided parent hand a bag of tacks to a bored eight-year-old. Of course, it's up to you to say just how many times you can hear Elvis thanking you very much, or Madonna informing you of what music does, before going mad. But these days the sound is turned off on more than a few computers before any chat is entered. And a lot of men like Elvis and Madonna less than they used to. And that's just a shame.

WHEN HE'S (REALLY) NOT ALONE

Here's a tip for when you come across a hot, familiar name online and wish to relive a wonderful scene of cyber lust with its owner: *Do not IM something graphic if you can tell that he is not actually in a chat room at the moment.* Yes, you may IM with a hi. But leave it at that. Sometimes, logged in or not, he isn't free. Sometimes the girlfriend or boyfriend really *is* right around the corner, and your guy had only a moment to jump on and do an e-mail check. And nothing will get him fuming more than a sudden spurt of dirty language on his monitor when, just then, Amber or Mom is a scant few yards away. It can be fun when worlds collide on a screen. But only when it's the latest video game.

Discreet testing of the waters is a courtesy you really need to practice, especially as many younger men employ the same screen name for all their online doings. That is to say, they don't take the time that more senior users take to isolate themselves for a romantic virtual interlude. The younger the guy, the more apt he is to jump from some quick research on a football team or apartment listings to a gay chat. Not infrequently he's got it all going on at the same time. And this usually means he's accessible to anyone or anything in his home at the time.

So keep that first hello clean. Keep it short. Believe it: If he's in the mood to play, he won't be shy about letting you know. Which is another great thing about younger guys.

IM ROLE-PLAYING: THE NEW—AND ALREADY LOST—ART

Whoever you want is exactly who
I'm more than willing to be.
—*"The Girl You Think You See," Carly Simon*

THERE ARE GUYS OUT THERE WHO RENEW OUR HOPE in the sense of fun and creativity men can still summon. No, they're not profile writers. They're the boys who enjoy cyber sex.

Cyber sex. It is too bad the name sounds as trashy as it does. The activity is, in fact, less sleazy than many another online tasks. And done well, it calls for imagination, passion, and quick thinking.

You will usually know indirectly when you have landed such an artist. He rarely announces his intent, although the more gracious will ask if you'd like to engage in a virtual session. He is as well marked by another distinction. Many a user will begin by getting hot and heavy in instant messaging, and then feverishly recommend you join him in a telephone conversation relating to the subject matter. Not our scene-player. For him, the joy is in the text.

He begins by transforming you both to an appropriate setting: the gym locker room, let's say. Combining the skill of a striptease artist with the eye of an especially gifted film director, he then paints a picture bursting with erotic possibilities. He is never crude. Not at first. Instead, he assigns you your part, and even this is customarily based upon the facts in your profile. A real pro, he has done his homework.

He tells you exactly what he is doing and wearing and feeling, and everything is set in the present tense, as well it should be. It's all about being "in the moment," as they say on *Inside the Actors Studio*. He is opening his locker after a vigorous workout, or game of basketball ("hoops," if he is younger than twenty-five). You enter the locker room. It is strangely deserted for a changing space adjacent to a just-finished event, but what the hell. This is what's called "suspension of disbelief" in arty circles.

His messages lose little time in adding all the necessary touches. He is tired, yes, but open to the possibilities of arousal. Often he has not had an active girlfriend in six months (six months apparently being the average duration of time before the most ardently heterosexual man can't take any more and opens his mind to other outlets). If he is a very gifted IM scene-player, he makes small talk with you. If he is brilliant—and some are, I swear—he so subtly weaves suggestion into the small talk that your cues are unmistakable. And in a really well-constructed episode, he will soon comment on the fact that you, Coach, are lookin' kinda funny at him. But he don't mind.

And on it goes. We will take it no further here, though. A critic can tell you in minute detail about the splendors of a Renaissance fresco, but it's not quite the same as visiting the church.

Now the bad news. Naturally, you must be in the proper frame of mind for this sort of ten- to fifteen-minute drama to work. It is not for the impatient, and many of us, online and alone, would really rather cut to the chase. Too bad, that. Perhaps we are all jaded by quick-fix media and find it hard to undertake the slower, but more rewarding, steps of the dance.

Then, too, you now have an impression of the real artist of the IM scene, but his breed is rare, and the ranks are getting slimmer everyday. What you will come across far more frequently is the hack, the fellow who approaches you with a message *sort of* scenic and who quickly warps all the laws of physics as his passion consumes him and he forgets, moment by moment, just where the two of you were supposed to be. He will start by emphatically insisting you join him in his fictive bathroom stall in the department store. You do, only to discover in his next message that you are now, in fact, in the back of a Greyhound bus. And you often ascertain this only by asking your fevered correspondent just what driver, checking the two of you out and licking his lower lip, he is suddenly referring to?

Worse than even these rustics, though, are the tedious wannabes. These are the primitives who give one lousy sentence for a setting, and then occupy the entirety of the rest of the exchange with strings of orders and cries of ecstasy. The hallmark of this most unevolved of the scenists? The comically extended chorus line of vowels in the orgasmic howl: "YEAH do it oooooooooooooh!!!!" One finger plied on a single spot for a considerable period of time may indeed produce good sensations. But not on a keyboard.

So, when you are targeted by and recognize the bad scene-player for what he is, get out of there. It is a world too half-assed in which to dwell, even within the little world of IM boxes. One recalls the old toast of the retired general to the elderly prostitute: "I give you, madame, the two oldest professions in history. Both of them ruined by amateurs."

WHEN YOU'RE DUMPED FROM AN IM . . . RELATIONSHIP

But fools will be fools, and where's he gone to?
—*"The Man That Got Away," Ira Gershwin and Harold Arlen*

THIS BREEZY LITTLE SYNDROME DESERVES ITS OWN chapter.

As previously noted, a kind of cyber chemistry can happen in a messaged dialogue, something above and beyond the connection forged by mutual desires. Yes, you both like doing this, and, better yet, he likes doing that just as much as you like having that done. But a different level of excitement can come into play on these occasions. I tend to think that cybernetic energy can, in a way not yet cataloged by science, carry more than the rudimentary, albeit lusty, remarks typed into a keyboard. Sometimes something of you is actually getting through to something of him, and it's fiery and more real than the mechanics of the situation should allow.

Let's say this goes on for days with a certain guy, at intermittent periods. It's still an enormous charge messaging with this guy, every time. It's kismet.

Then he's gone.

You don't know why, how, or where. You are, in essence, a version of the female stereotypically dumped after the first great date. He may have changed his screen name, his wife may have taken an ax to his computer, he may have gotten ill, he may have blocked you, he may have developed a case of amnesia to rival that of a soap opera character. It doesn't matter. You are lost. And befuddled and truly hurt.

REALITY CHECK

Here's the thing to remember: If you honestly felt that something transcending normal messaging was going on, it was. You can't ever know what happened, but you must trust what you *do* know. The contact would never have been prolonged if you weren't doing as much for him as he was for you. It ended, yes, and not by your choice. But perhaps, as in real life, it is better this way. Perhaps there was nowhere else for it to go, and you are now spared the ugliness of watching it die.

Take comfort in the high seas. Rich with meaning through seemingly destined navigational proximity, or just plain temporarily adjacent, ships really do pass in the night.

GETTING SERIOUS:
THE PERSONAL ADS

BEFORE YOU PLACE ONE . . .

Everybody's hard as iron
Dreams are made of a different stuff.
—"Method of Modern Love," Daryl Hall and John Oates

IF YOU HAVE A LOGICAL MIND, IT MAY WELL OCCUR TO you that rather than waste hours in the quagmires of the chat rooms, it is far more sensible to simply place a personal ad. Those on the better sites are perused by millions daily, after all. Why sit by the stream, slapping mosquitoes and stifling yawns, when all you need to do is put your order in at the fish market?

Well, you are right. You are wrong, too, but that is no great surprise.

Everything online, particularly in the spheres of romantic and/or sexual mating, serves only to augment everything else in that sphere. No single approach is the best one, and even a combination of the best may yield mixed results. If one avenue guaranteed success in the field of romance—or even hooking-up—you can safely assume the rest would vanish from the Internet through nonuse, and pretty quickly.

REALITY CHECK

Running a personal ad brings no assurance of success. You knew that. You may even slightly resent a piece of counsel so clearly evident and needless. But look, and look hard, at these words. There is *no guarantee* of success. Your ad may be honest and beautiful and even sexy, as you yourself may be. But it may very well fail to draw to you he whom you desire. Because he whom you desire might be with another guy, or not really into you. Just like in life.

The good news? Something like a billion men are out there looking too. Never before in mankind's history of seeking love—which probably dates back to mankind's first hour on the planet—have there been numbers like these to mix and mingle with. The newspaper personal of a few years ago was intimidating for many because previously unheard-of masses were being targeted to fulfill erotic or romantic dreams. Compared to the number of men reachable on the Internet, that old print ad today is about as effective as a message in a bottle, tossed into the ocean.

And the sites keep piling on. As the supply increases, so does the demand, it seems. So take heart. Love is a tricky thing at best. But the odds of finding something close to it are very much in your favor, and getting better every day.

THE SITES

THERE ARE CONFLICTING OPINIONS ABOUT WHICH personals site is best. Naturally. But for our purposes, we will look at what I feel are the Big Three: Yahoo.com, Gay.com, and the full-steam-ahead site Cruisingforsex.com.

Each represents a certain style, a mode of presentation and offerings geared to a relatively specific gay-dating mind-set. Each may parallel other sites, some of which are megasites indeed. OutPersonals.com, for instance, may dwarf Yahoo! Personals in subscription numbers, and the dizzying rise of Manhunt.net's popularity must surely be giving Gay.com a run for its money. Yet our Big Three are chosen because they are like the primary colors on the color wheel: Manhunt.net is a little bit Gay.com and a whole lot of Cruisingforsex.com; OutPersonals.com is a Yahoo! that can't keep its zipper up. So let's turn to our Big Three, knowing that what we need to know about all the others can be gleaned from them.

(Note: The opinions rendered here are based wholly on my own experiences with each and input from multiple sources also acquainted with them and/or subscribers to them. These opinions are in no way colored by any sort of relationship with any of the referred-to sites.)

YAHOO! PERSONALS

This is the nice one. Yahoo! is the one most in sync with AOL's feverish belief in nothing but a wholesome bunch of users out there. When you go to Yahoo! Personals, you don't need to dress up. But you really should be wearing something other than a T-shirt, and your pants should be on and zipped. The Yahoo! Personals vibe is, and always has been, for the guy after something meaningful, if only for friendship.

Moving with the times, however, Yahoo! now acknowledges that maybe it isn't all about lasting relationships. When you now investigate the signing-up procedure, two options await you; one is simpler, for "casual dating" purposes, and the other is for those after the real thing. For the latter, a "relationship test" is suggested, and the names of the next two steps give you some idea of how serious Yahoo! expects you to be. "Find Other Hopeful Romantics" is the second phase, and they don't hold back on employing the words "marriage material." Go this path, and you'll wind up ready to "Start Something Meaningful." And despite bowing to fast-love devotees, this is still really what Yahoo! is all about.

One sticky issue with this site is the photography department. Uploading and displaying your pictures here aren't a walk in the park. Now, many of us *do* need to be taken by the hand through these kinds of procedures, and would run into snags no matter how simple the site made the chore. But even web-smart guys get into trouble with Yahoo! because it appears to have a discretionary darkroom. I have been informed by more than one subscriber that Yahoo! Personals rejects or modifies photographs. You send along one you obviously think is flattering, a nice head-and-torso shot taken on vacation; Yahoo!, a hopped-up Henry VIII, slices off your head and blows it up into an unrecognizable oval of fuzzy. You upload that picture of yourself running with a kite in the park; Yahoo! crops it so that the kite seems to be the one searching for company. However it happens at Yahoo!, it doesn't happen easily.

Of course, these glitches may be no more than minor foibles within Yahoo!'s programming. They may in fact be history, even as this is written. I merely record the frustrations encountered by the men who looked for love yonder and who, frustrated, vented in my direction. That aside, the man looking for male companionship on Yahoo! is best served if he is of the moonlight-stroll-on-the-beach ilk. Read a few Yahoo! postings. In a little while it will occur to you that the lonely Yahoo! subscriber need not waste his time with an ad. All he has to do is wait until dark and head for the shoreline. He can't possibly begin to feel sand between his toes before bumping into a like-minded man.

This is of course equally true of the similar—can I say Yahooey? I really want to—sites out there. You will know them by their discretion, and most definitely by the absence of the down-and-dirty. These are the sites that believe in love.

Which is fine, really. It just usually means, as it means in life, that having a hobby or two with which to occupy yourself while you wait for it isn't a bad idea.

GAY.COM

Gay.com, favorite son of the PlanetOut family, is something of a force to be reckoned with. Ads; chat rooms; politically charged articles; discounts for gay-focused travel, film, and music reviews; pornography—the whole of gay life in bytes and banners. It is to the gay scene what Universal Studios is to theme parks. If you want it and it ain't here, your appetites need examining.

The Gay.com chat rooms deserve a serious mention before we look at the site's personals. These are some admirably executed chats. For one thing, newcomers to the specific rooms automatically go to the top of the list, so you are spared the nuisance of forever scrolling down to scout out newcomers to the space. Would that AOL chats were so structured. (AOL's notion of improving chat a few years ago was to set it up so that new chatters are perpetually shuffled in alphabetically. It is annoying as hell. The minor advantage gained of knowing just where to locate that name you like—never especially a problem to begin with given the small square of twenty to thirty-five names to scroll through—hardly compensates for incessant shuffling of the deck. You have the sense in a busy AOL chat of a neurotic housekeeper endlessly putting the magazines on the coffee table in just the right order.)

Another plus with Gay.com chats is that pictures are aligned with names. It is, granted, quite literally a small plus; the photos adjacent to the members' names are as clear and large as an ultrasound image of a fetus in its second week in utero. And you won't be seeing any enlargements of photos on the *site's* dime, thank you; only subscribers enjoy that privilege. In addition, many a man there still chooses to remain invisible. Nonetheless, it is still a helpful feature. If you can squint. And frequently you are at least saved the extra clicking of opening a profile in the hope that GYMJCKnUrTown provided a nice shirtless image of himself.

And the personals? Well done, well done. For no fee at all, you can set up a very comprehensive profile of yourself, complete with multiple photos and descriptive text about how much you drink and how many tattoos you sport. All right, the questionnaire *is* a little lengthy and strangely arbitrary. Gay.com doesn't just want your political leanings here; it wants to know where you're pierced, too. And with what.

But why quibble? The fact remains, at Gay.com, you can safely and thoroughly billboard yourself among the more than 6.5 million members the site astonishingly claims to possess, and for free. You won't be seeing the "adult" photos of other members, though. Not unless you pony up $19.95 a month (or go for the bargain, a full year at $89 and change). Nor can you do lots of other things, such as read the more prurient preferences listed in the ads you admire, reply to them, or—and I love the "privileged classes" aspect to this—jump right into an already full chat room, as a premium subscriber may. The choice, as the Internet lives to proclaim, is yours. You can choose to not pay for premium membership at Gay.com and you may very well get lucky, or even get love. But if you spend serious online time in the pursuit of men, the price ain't bad, the options are many, and 6.5 million men is nothing to sneeze at.

CRUISINGFORSEX.COM

Finally, there is Cruisingforsex.com. Gentlemen, start your engines.

There's a lot to like about this site. There is no pretense to spirituality here, as you may safely discern from the name. LTRs, romance, even compatibility in recreational pursuits—not in these parts, boys. If love is a battlefield, Cruisingforsex.com is the front line.

The home page is daunting, and best viewed unaccompanied. Ads for porn movies and for the promotions of the site's own many and graphic features are displayed here, with no blurring of what on other sites, unless you subscribe, gets blurred. But in the midst of this sea of pornographic enticements are links to some very excellent hunting grounds. There is the worldwide listings feature. This, believe me, is something. It is a sort of eBay of male sex without the prices. It's all about feedback, and there's an enormous amount of it. For years comments, raves, and warnings about the best places to find gay sex have been carefully woven into a smutty tapestry that does, indeed, cover the world.

Interestingly, an element of political awareness has had to make itself felt in these otherwise purely sporty pages. As gay sex conducted in public places is of course illegal—and the site does not hesitate to inform the cruiser of the risks involved in any such activity—various arrests occur in various places, and usually during mayoral campaigns. The site then offers up a hearty "Heads up!" under these circumstances, when a contributing cruiser, or even a report in the press, points to increased police vigilance in a particular neighborhood. The political factor lies in the intrinsic harassment of gaydom, of course. Straight people, generally speaking, don't need to resort to alleyways and mall restrooms for sexual gratification, and are thus spared the handcuffs. Courtesy of the checks and balances of the universe, however, they miss out on a great deal of fun, too.

A word of caution about these listings: In the human animal, and most assuredly in the gay human animal, there is a tendency to embellish. So you will read accounts of encounters more thrilling than any filmed by the most creative porn producer, followed by posts registering utter disbelief that such ecstasy transpired in that setting. Some people lie. Some are luckier than others, or their timing is better. Take it all with as much salt as you can digest. You might be swayed by a string of rapturous paragraphs regarding a Southern bookstore. You might go. And you might come away empty, hot as you are. That does not necessarily mean you were a sucker for some fancy storytelling. It's far more likely that your timing was unlucky. As they say in France, *c'est la guerre*.

Beyond the listings, Cruisingforsex.com does as much as it can to promote interaction through other means. Anyone can place an ad in their "Communal Stalls" section, charmingly christened after that nexus of clandestine homosexual romping, the public bathroom. And they may be as graphic as they please within this ad, provided they steer very, very clear from blatantly racist remarks or references to minors. So too does the site boast an immense and ceaselessly active message board. All cities; all states; all countries, for that matter: If you want to tell the world what you need, how you need it, and where you'll be on March 9 to get it, then this, friend, is the venue.

In case the options put forth so far are too genteel, there is the Instant Sex feature. (The name itself is appealing in an old-fashioned way, like "Snapshots in a Minute!") This is the section in which you compose the kind of profile AOL is in strenuous denial about. You may upload photo after photo, each displaying more flagrantly just why you deserve as much sex as can be had. As elsewhere on the site, men from every corner of the globe are represented, and represented . . . fully.

Ever reinventing the mousetrap, Cruisingforsex.com enhances this vibrant area with a "Who's On Now" link. Click the appropriate button and see who else is at his desk right then, most probably clicking to see you—in your town, in New Zealand, in Ecuador. Ultimately, if Cruisingforsex.com is any indication of the numbers of men seeking fast sex, it really is a jungle out there. And nearly every vine is taken.

REALITY CHECK

If you believe that all you need to do is sign on, upload, and get down, you're in for some disappointment. Know this, and know it well: Even the very best cyber site for sex or dating is nothing more than an excessively fragmented bar. The reality is still unchanged, regardless of the astronomical numbers. You may come up empty. Just as you may search through thousands of ceramic ashtrays on eBay and still, unaccountably, not find the right one. Or lose the bid. Hot men, not hot men, endless combinations of both, and in the most active corners yet to be discovered, and we all still, time and again, drive home alone.

But that's quite enough cautioning. There are, again, very many sites. There's JockBod.com, BigMuscle.com, and all their multifaceted kin, which strive to unite buff with buff in a kind of specialized breeding pen. A quick Google search and about three hundred pages will line up, each offering links to dozens of new and not-so-new gay dating arenas. One site exists to match up potential "houseboys" with "employers," and it is *jammed* with subscribers. Another, newer pay service caters to the executive, out to connect him only with other men of substantial means, solid levels of prestige, and really expensive bed linens. In addition, there are far more dating sites that are less sexually aggressive; they are the cousins of the amiable Yahoo! giant. It truly appears, in fact, that the single most in-demand consumer item on the market today is other consumers. If only for an hour or so.

There's a bright side you need to be aware of. There had to be one, or a lot fewer men would be making their fortunes as gay dating site webmasters. And this bright side is almost blinding. There are literally millions and millions of men with ads placed online. That's the fact of it. As previously stated in an effort to play down unrealistic expectations, the net is one big virtual gay bar. But this bar is big, brother, very big. It is almost unimaginably enormous. True, love is hard to find under any circumstances. A date, though, or even some fast company, comes easier, and these sites empower you to get one or get some to no end.

YOU CALL THIS A RÉSUMÉ?: PUTTING YOUR AD TOGETHER

THE PROFILE YOU PUT UP FOR CHAT ROOM PURPOSES is the barbecue in the backyard; the ad you place on the personals site is dinner out, and at the place with the good linen.

Wherein lies the upgrade? First of all, you're probably paying for the opportunity to set up the personals ad, and paying for anything adds import. Second, it's understood that *the degree of intent with both poster and responder usually varies with the online activity chosen.* The guy jumping into a chat room may be out for some fast self-gratification, a little entertainment, or a semierotic, semiamusing way to kill ten minutes at the office. But the guy scanning the personals has a plan. He is most definitely out for something, and you may be it. Furthermore, as far as the personal ads go on any site at all, there are only so many for the region in which he's searching. He knows this. Make no mistake: Your ad is going to be read with special care.

So let's get into what to get into it. Much of what you see below will be reminiscent of the profile instructions. This is unavoidable, as either a profile or an ad is—excuse the cynicism—a sales pitch in the market of love. But the stakes are higher here. When you take out the personal ad online, you're turning up the heat. So the advice here is that much more focused.

- Right off the bat, let's jack up the volume on a tip given for profiles: the photo. For a chat room profile, it's recommended but it remains your call. With a personal ad it's essential. And you want more than one, even if you're aiming more for the heart and north of the waist. Remember what was bellowed earlier: No matter how personality driven the man investigating you appears to be, *what you look like* will determine just how attractive your personality is to him. In a perfect world we'd none of us care about appearance. On this sphere, we do. All of us.

- Whether to use more than one photo is dependent on the ad you're running and where it runs. An especially clear, full face shot is a good idea if you're doing the Yahoo! character-based rounds. Remember, though, our looks don't end at our necks. Post that picture of yourself in shorts on the deck. If you want someone to fall in love with you, let him see all of what he's falling for.

If, however, you've chosen to set yourself out on the meat racks of the Cruisingforsex.com genre, you know what you need to provide. Doing so may not be elegant. It may not even enhance your self-esteem. But when you play at this casino, all cards on the table, gents.

• Don't hedge. Say what you're after, and say it straight out. To begin with, hedging wastes time and space. Then going off on a tangent of the variables you *might* consider in a date/friend/one-nighter is asking for trouble. Understand that the man interested in your ad will already be doing some serious yoga to make himself fit into the parameters you lay out, should he fall a little short of your designated desires. An expressed relaxing of your standards, even with the nonphysical inclinations, and it's Thunderdome. Anything goes, and you let it happen.

• Use examples of what you're looking for whenever possible. Don't say that your dream guy is slender, boyish, and equipped with a devilish gleam in his otherwise innocent eye; say that you like a Matt Damon type. Delete whatever you wrote about how a sense of humor just knocks you out; there are far, far too many kinds of senses of humor, and most of them aren't funny. Instead, cite a movie or a book known to pretty much all. (TV shows are tricky; everyone loves *Seinfeld*, for example, so a reference to the show does nothing to pinpoint your own tastes. Saying that *Lost* cracks you up, however . . . now, that just may do it. You'd certainly get a response from me.)

• Omit any and all references to finding someone for life. If a real relationship is what you're after, fine. Nobody's mocking the ambition—it lies within most of us. But to spell out the longing in your ad carries with it a lot of implications, and most of them aren't attractive.

First and foremost, and no matter how confidently it's phrased, stating that you seek a substantial partner is just too daunting to a stranger, which is what the man reading your ad is. Translate the experience to a club. Interesting guy saunters over, you strike up a conversation, and things are going along very well. Would you then tell him that you are in search of someone to spend your life with? Only if a more interesting guy was looking your way and you wanted to free up that bar stool.

Keep your intent to find Mr. Right where it belongs: to yourself. It should, after all, have that dignity attached to it. As long as you convey that you are open to something developing between you both, should any initial encounters prove worthwhile, you've conveyed plenty.

• Before you compose the text of your ad, think about the ones you yourself find most compelling. Not in terms of types, say, or even romantic goals, but in presentation.

The man who proclaims in his personal ad that he wants a future with someone is lessening his own desirability, and in a big way, because he's revealing an unspoken and arrogant belief in his own suitability to be partnered up for life, no matter what the other guy brings to the party. It doesn't matter that he would certainly adapt to a potential boyfriend's needs; the potential boyfriend is reading the words of someone who clearly thinks *he's* ready as is. And we all know that none of us is nearly as ready as we think we are.

You'll notice a pattern, an appealing and direct style of address to them. Do likewise.

- As in profile writing, *keep it brief*. With every passing day, we are all less tolerant of huge blocks of copy on the screen; A lot of images and very few words is much more effective. In this respect, the harshness of the Internet is a very good writing coach indeed. It demands economy in prose. If the words aren't necessary to what you need to say, cut them.

- Just as you shouldn't hedge with what you're looking for, be direct with what you yourself are. This is pretty easy when it comes to your age, physicality, and appearance/style. It gets hazier when we're talking about your character. . . .

> Are you funny? Do people tend to laugh robustly at your remarks? Great. But you don't want to say that. What you want to convey is that you *find humor* in a lot of what life hands you. And you want to give a (short) example, preferably woven into your text: "My sense of humor is pretty strong. Hey, I'm placing this ad, after all." Or, "I like guys with a solid sense of humor. As long as they don't laugh at my naked pics." All right, not exactly riotously funny. But you get the idea. And trust me— the ad with a touch of genuine self-deprecating humor goes far, indeed, in attracting men, if only because it stands out so boldly from all the too severe, too full-of-themselves ads.

> If you're the type of man who spends more time outdoors than inside, say so, and say it big; this is an important, defining preference. For example, "If we meet up for coffee the first time and it goes great, I'll want to go hiking on the next date." Or, "When I say 'the great outdoors,' I'm not kidding. It's my life." In either example, your potential date will know that his idea of a long, lazy happy hour in a gloomy bar most likely won't fly with you.

> If your ad is sexually focused and you don't want to ever go beyond that range, spell it out. Remember, the wise placer of a sex ad who maybe wants something long-lasting won't be blowing his chances by saying so; conversely, leaving your *sex* ad open-ended—so to speak—paints you just as potentially available for romance: "NOT seeking a relationship, men. Sorry, but it's only about a good time with me." Of course, this is in itself bait for the LTR seeker. Your heart isn't out there for the taking, so a lot of men will want to take it even more. But you're covered, having been *unequivocally* honest.

• Important, and often neglected: *Make sure any interested guy can contact you.* Most personals sites offer varying degrees of membership; the free variety usually permits the browsing of ads, but won't let you respond to one unless you join that fabulous site. Know what your site permits and doesn't permit, and learn it as an outsider would. If a nonsubscriber's hands are tied, get your e-mail into the ad.

• Do *not* post your ad upon completion. Let it sit for a spell, like a pie cooling on a windowsill. Have another look later that day, or the next. Edit some more.

• If intensely raunchy sex is your goal, swell. But don't take the pointless and unattractive step of listing all that comprises, to

you, intensely raunchy sex. A few synonyms for "raunchy"—
or even just that one word, really—will tell the world where
you're at, and that it's not bingo night at the local VFW
hall.

• By all means, set down the physicality of the man you'd
like to be with. By *no* means catalog all that's unacceptable
to you. As with the profile, it's fine to say you're interested
only in men thirty-five or younger; it's adolescent, rude, and
redundant to say "NO ONE over thirty-five!"

RESPONSES, REJECTIONS, REVISIONS, RESULTS

OKAY. YOU'VE TAKEN THE TROUBLE TO WRITE A COOL, engaging ad. It says what you need it to say, it doesn't say too much, and it's got that one really terrific picture of you to send it over the top. You've clicked on all the right buttons to make it live. You breathe deeply, and with satisfaction. Your ad is running.

What follows? Pick one:

A) It's running, all right. Unfortunately, it's running in the way that a horse stuck at the Aqueduct starting gate is running. Four days, five days, two weeks later, and not one response.

B) It's running amok. Somehow, it's attracting to your mailbox at least several examples of all the types you specifically don't want to meet up with.

C) It's running at a nice, steady gallop. There are responses, and they're kind of interesting. This is what you did it for, and it's happening.

More than one issue may be responsible. Rethink the process.

- Are you there to begin with? Have you gone into the site as an outsider and seen your own listing? Don't laugh. There are quite a few users who, after hours of intense ad composition, fail to make one vital click and remain in cyber limbo. And no kindly old clerk is at his desk at the website's headquarters, wiping his spectacles and carefully ensuring that your ad is properly up. They got your money. Your exposure is your responsibility, provided all their instructions are clearly set out.

- Are you in the right place? That is, have you selected the personals site best suited to your wants and to what you have to offer? Look over the ads you see there again; if most of them are directly sexually oriented and your own ad expresses less sweaty aims, you didn't do your homework before you signed up.

- This is the most unlikely, but possible: is your ad hopelessly unclear?

    Let's look at a guy posting in a sexually driven site. He's fortyish and eager to find a younger boy to spank. This—with a good picture—would do it:

    "Fortysomething 'dad,' good-looking, works out—46 chest, 34 wst, 5'11", 210 lbs—wants a hot boy who enjoys a little dad/son role-play and dad's hand on his ass when he's bad. No kink, freaks, minors." This wouldn't: "Where's my bad boy? Daddy needs you—punishment = love, and it's all good when a boy trusts his daddy."

You've seen these ads. Not good. First off, just whom exactly is to be punished? Second, there's something creepy going on here; is he talking about spanking or electroshock? The hot boy won't respond because the ad implies extreme behavior, and the extremist/S&M devotee won't respond because it's too ambiguous—clearly a sign of the amateur—and because there's a suggestion of affection.

REALITY CHECK

Any expert on website design worth his salt will tell you in no uncertain terms that the most essential thing you can do is keep it simple and direct. Don't make the user think, because he doesn't want to. This strategy translates to the personal ad. You are selling yourself. The product, then, deserves the cleanest, clearest presentation possible.

WHEN "B" OCCURS . . .

There's pretty much only one reason. Bad ad, bad ad.

Yes, even the most lucid personals attract the wrong types.

But when absolutely everyone knocking at your door belongs down the block, the fault, dear Brutus, is in yourself. And it involves one or more of the five deadly sins of personal ad composition:

1. **Vagueness.** E.g., "caring soul" instead of "sane, friendly guy," or "wild sex partner" instead of "real, masculine top."

   There are wild sex partners who like near-suffocation. This may not be exactly what you were after.

2. **Poetry.** "Here is my heart, as open to love as the meadow grasses are to the sweet caress of the summer sun . . ."

   The meadow, friend, will be scoring. You won't.

3. **Aggression.** "I'm fed up with all the sick losers contacting me. One more an' I'm comin' outta this screen to kick your sorry ass."

   Charming in a feisty, murderous sort of way. But I'll pass.

4. **Lamenting.** "How much longer do I need to be alone?!?"

   Oh, quite a while. Quite a while.

5. **Bitterness.** "Liars. Liars and fakes. NO ONE is real—are you????"

   Uh . . . guess not.

Once more—*edit your ad*. Keep in mind the cardinal rule of the online personal:

The ad should be as agreeable, as direct, and as encouraging as the best guy you met at the best party you ever went to. Edit. Go forth, and waste words no more.

WHEN "C" HAPPENS . . .

Everything is grand. You placed a terrific ad and you're getting some terrific responses. But success isn't without its burdens. You still have work to do. . . .

Do I Need to Reply to Everyone Who Writes Me?

Unless you're generating more online activity than eBay, yes.

Don't look like that, like you've just been told that the report you haven't started yet has to be in perfect shape by Monday, and have a great weekend. Remember, we're generally talking about *good* responses here. These are the guys you sought out. For whatever reason you don't think some or most of them aren't worth the investment of your returned interest isn't their fault. You issued the invitation; you should acknowledge the responses.

Keep your rejections short, friendly, and socially adept:

• Hey, Tom. Thanks for the contact. Not sure we'd hit it off, though—I was looking more for a _____ kind of guy. Take care, and good luck.

- Hey, Tom. You sound great, but I'm more into _____ just now. Best to you.

- Hey, Tom. Great note, thanks. Still dealing with responses here—I'll get back to you soon, okay?

Now, the last example seems a little dangerous. It's open-ended, and for some reason you don't want to see this man in your mailbox again. But the cost of *many* a civil rejection is renewed, stubborn attempts. If Tom doesn't get that you're sending him a thanks-but-no-thanks—and a lot of Toms won't, even if you were to be far more abrupt—he will be back regardless. But having been initially courteous, you are entirely off the hook. You did the right thing, and can thereafter ignore.

How Can I Trust the Honesty of These Guys?

You can't. That is, you can't any more than they can trust your own veracity. Which nicely leads us to . . .

How Much Scrutiny and Correspondence Is Appropriate Before We Meet?

The levels will vary with each responder, and what will determine those levels are:

- Number one, and for a reason: *your gut*. Does this reply feel real? Is it so naturally attractive that you've lost the sense of actually being online, and feel as though you've just "met" someone you'd like to know better? In this case, carry on with confidence. A few cyber back and forths, and you should be standing on solid ground. When your instincts about a connection are feeling this good, there's less need to waste time with investigating his character, his background, and his intentions.

- His picture. We know it looks pretty good to you—he wouldn't have potential otherwise. But is it holding anything back? A picture doesn't tell a thousand words. A picture tells a trillion words, and the face and body captured are by no means the whole tale. Stance, clothing, even background setting reveal untold amounts of data that we pick up and digest both consciously and unconsciously. It may be nothing much at all: a too-intent look to the eye, an aggressive posture, even something strange in the background. Whatever it is, it's giving you pause. And you may not be able to reconcile this snag through even a hundred online or telephone exchanges.

  In this instance, the meeting in public at the coffee bar is damn near mandatory.

Bill was delighted with the picture he received in response to his ad. The guy was completely Bill's type: he was youthful, he was handsome in a not-too-pretty way, and his posture—as depicted outside an admittedly hazy club of sorts—was confident and friendly. Was there something about the picture nagging at Bill, something he wasn't fully comfortable with but couldn't put his finger on? Yes. But he let it go. The date was set.

The date was short, as well. For the handsome young man had a tattoo around his neck, and in the photo this had looked like a chain. The hazy club, it turned out, was a pretty rough biker hangout. Now, Bill did not harbor any specific prejudices against bikers, neck tattoos, or bikers *with* neck tattoos. But this was also not exactly his element, either, and it created for Bill a sense of danger he would really rather have avoided.

So two things actually worked to render this a mistake of a contact. The first was Bill's ignoring a disturbing aspect of the picture and subsequently neglecting to follow up and get a little more background before arranging the date. And the second was the affable biker's failure to indicate something about a lifestyle not usually in sync with most other people's, which was a very real responsibility on his part.

- How insistent is he that you get together, and fast? We don't care how Joe Right he appears to be; too much urgency is a red flag. It bespeaks a level of desperation, and that's never a good element to bring to the table.

  If you're feeling too pressured way too early, test it. The more he insists, the more you should hold back a little. Don't cave in just to placate. There are too many online daters who *bully* men into meeting, for the sole purpose of going through as many men as possible. And if he gets even more demanding after you've expressed a natural reluctance or sense of caution, whack your horse on the ass and head for the hills.

- Conversely, if he's just a bit too apathetic about actually getting together after a solid period of online and/or telephone acquaintance, give it two, and no more than two, tries. If your communication thus far is solid and enjoyable, and if he still fudges about a real-life encounter after you've suggested a mutually accommodating one for the second time, you need to think about moving on. No one is *that* busy, after all.

- Ultimately, if the guy is great, you're both excited at having found each other online, and there are no geographic impediments, you should be able to arrange an honest-to-God meeting after merely a few e-mails or IM chats. All other admonitions aside, if the process is dragging beyond this, something somewhere is telling you it is not meant to be. Don't go mad seeking out the mysterious culprit. Read the first bullet point in this list again; its value is incalculable. *Trust your instincts.*

BEYOND ONLINE

PHONE SEX:
THE CALLS OF THE WILD

I want to talk like lovers do.
—*"Here Comes the Rain Again," Eurythmics*

PHONE SEX IS PRECISELY WHAT YOU THINK IT IS. IT IS conversation conducted on the telephone between two parties who wish to achieve sexual excitement and—presumably—climax through the content of the dialogue.

The activity most certainly didn't originate strictly as a gay male thing. It may be the one facet of a commonly gay sexual practice invented, or at least made popular, by straight guys and girls. For before computers graced every home, everybody knew about those 900 numbers that delivered, for $5.99 per minute, a frumpy housewife in Duluth, Minnesota, pretending to be a busty and wanton chick in LA. These were, and still are, a big business. And there are plenty of otherwise perfectly respectable women who occasionally please their men by means of the good people at Verizon or BellSouth.

No matter who first dialed a number to get off and for no other purpose; it didn't take long for mastery of phone sex to become yet another jewel on the gay crown. By its very nature, it belongs to us. It is furtive, and done when no one else is hanging about the house. It is completely anonymous. You could, if push came to shove, try describing your partner in it to a third party. But odds are, you will be wide of the mark as far as real accuracy goes.

Phone sex. It merits a chapter because it is not unrelated to the online world we are dealing with. It is, in fact, a hefty limb on the gay cyber tree. You won't be online long before such a request—ordinarily phrased simply as "fone?"—pops up at you in an IM. You will also see, when you scan the dialogue screen of the chat, a liberal peppering of such queries closing the sentences in which your fellow cruisers relay their hot stats. The technology of interactive sex has moved on, but the old-fashioned phone call remains in the game. It still has its place. Bring back the Concordes and let the people fly to defy sound. The trains will nonetheless roll down their ancient tracks, too.

REALITY CHECK

Phone sex is a state of limbo between pornography and actual sex, a shadowy dimension where things are somewhat real and not real at all. It is sex between two people with absolutely no responsibility, no aftermath, no pre-love ritual, and little in the way of cleanup afterward. All both parties need to bring to the table is desire, a willingness to talk and be heard, and a telephone.

JACK MAURO

I salute phone sex. As with IM role-playing, it's a refreshingly low-tech means to an end replete with too many other, less creative, routes to it. It reassures us that no high-speed download, no latest release from the artists at Falcon, Colt, or Jackrabbit productions can match the excitement generated by a husky voice talking dirty in the ear.

It isn't exactly easy, however. First, there's the time issue. It is a paramount support for the institution of phone sex. If the wife, girlfriend, or boyfriend runs to the market for ten minutes, what better way is there to get a quick fix? You could of course jump online and fulfill your urgent need via a few selections from the myriad dirty pictures and films clips piled up there. But that won't always do. Sometimes the verbal connection is imperative, and you have only a very narrow window in which to make it happen.

The good phone sex practitioner also must be quick to adapt to the *other* guy's time constraints, as well as his sexual needs. Phone sex isn't exactly love, but it requires quite a bit of the same sort of give-and-take. And provided the callers avail themselves of ID-privacy safeguards, it is as safe as it gets for the not openly bisexual, curious, or repressed and married fellow. With only the telephone used as the instrument of passion, and with his number blocked, his security is inviolable.

REALITY CHECK

> Phone sex between strangers who met online almost never goes beyond the phone. No matter how intently both parties enjoy the experience, no matter how long the phone relationship lasts, the experience intrinsically belongs exclusively to the cell or the landline because the whole thing is built on unreality, on fantasy, on the invisible.

We live in the video age, to be sure. We are damn near intolerant of anything not whirling before our jaded eyes. And as lustful gratification goes, this medium caters to a dizzying array of sexual tastes. But it doesn't stop there; this is the *personal* video age. The digital camera found in most homes permits all the individual image recording one's heart requires, and these images are traded online at a fever pitch to rival Wall Street on a particularly crazed afternoon. So you might think the webcam would render phone sex obsolete. After all, why just hear when you can see, too? Why bother setting up a call with a hot man when even hotter men have cameras perched on their computers?

Because the webcam encounter, while also of the netherworld between real and not real, is a perilous inch closer to the real. It demands much that the phone sex episode does nicely without: the visibly naked you. Don't misunderstand, you may be quite nice-looking. You may have nothing at all to be ashamed of when the knickers come off; you may even have a lot to flaunt, in which case anyone would suppose you would be hooking a webcam to the top of your computer within minutes of plugging it in.

But hot or not, video performance—and performance is *exactly* what a webcam scenario requires—is simply not everyone's bag. It is, in fact, the bag of relatively few. Just closing your eyes and listening, however—ah, there's a happy lull steeped in tradition! And the absence of the visual component adds just the right barrier. He is talking dirty, you are talking dirty back. But he can't see you. Yes, you've traded pictures, and each of you has a static image to manipulate, to play with, in your minds. Yet this provides only a limited pornographic element, easily adapted through imagination to become what the dialogue needs it to become. No one is live on the air. Therefore, you are not truly real, neither is he, and nothing essentially intimate is going on.

Moreover, the webcam is elitist. The visual component is its foundation, if not its sole attraction, and this leaves little room for the not impressively hot, whereas our friend Mr. Telephone is for all. This very egalitarianism may repulse you, if only on principle. You may have no intention of ever exchanging lurid words with an unattractive dude. You would rather attend to business without any outside stimuli, than get all hot and bothered on the phone with someone who may be homely.

If this is how you feel, then the realm of phone sex is not for you. It is not a place for the too literal minded. Remember, it's all about suspension of disbelief. If the guy *told* you online he was hot, and if the guy *sounds* hot on the phone, and a voice—with a well-timed concluding grunt—is what you're both after, then he's hot enough.

A note about who's calling whom: The more experienced practitioners of the—well, let's say "craft," not "art"—of phone sex take advantage of the ID block. Some are primarily straight or live with unsuspecting boyfriends and understandably unwilling to have their number in the hands of someone who may, in a fever of passion, call at the wrong time and ask the wife or boyfriend if she's still wearing that jockstrap. Others are out but share the understandable inclination to keep certain activities nicely apart from others, in terms of communication and otherwise. So you will often see "Restricted ID" on your phone's LCD display upon answering the call agreed upon a moment ago.

This can make you feel snubbed before the conversation even takes place. Don't be offended. These are strange times we live in, regarding privacy. You must exercise care. And guys who need barricades are always, always sexier.

Let's take a look at the basic phone sex devotees. If you play at all in this dark arena, you are going to be speaking to several, if not all, of them.

THE HOWLER

This gentleman is something else. Talk to him only when you are free to get very, *very* loud, because he fully expects you to match him in vocal power and abandon. He is outrageously over the top, bellowing commands and grunts, verbally switching positions and tasks with the agility of a Cirque de Soleil gymnast. Yet this in itself adds a winning charm. He usually fakes the climax, but he is so damn enthusiastic, that's just fine. And his strong suit is the multiple orgasm. If what you're hearing on the phone is to be believed, his heart should give out within a minute of the call's termination.

THE CORPSE

Strange beast, the Corpse. He is often the one to request that you carry over your IM chat to the phone. Yet once engaged, he appears to be so bored that you think about suggesting a game of checkers to liven things up. No matter that he was turned on by the text you had sent; something since then has made him inert. You are tempted to take it up a notch to refire his ardor with more aggressive tactics. Don't waste your time. Hanging up on someone is never a decent thing to do, but there are those who leave you with no alternative—especially when the line is, all things considered, dead already.

This fellow may sometimes be initially mistaken for the Corpse. But they are as distinctly different as different can be. One is an annoying waste of time; the other is the promised land. The Straight Guy transmits his authenticity in every nervous or cocky syllable. You will know him from the false straight guy through his ordinary tone, his hesitancy, his unintentionally revealed ignorance of the mechanics, and more. He will be nervous and shy. The false straight man is never this subtle; he believes a butch growl and assertiveness of manner will take you in. He is a blowup cowboy doll compared to the real thing.

When you get the real thing, know that it won't last very long. Truly straight guys dipping a toe into forbidden sex in this way have a lot of repression to explode, and not a lot of time. The final exam for Straight Guyness is the climax. Here is where you will know beyond question what kind of man is about to hang up, because his is beautifully nontheatrical. He gets there like most men do in real life: no screams of ecstasy, no roars of triumph. Just a satisfied gulp of air, a deep exhalation, and it's done. The sheer reality of this barely heard event can be a hundred times more exciting than the bellow of the best phone sex performer. As with the great IM role-players, you are unquestionably there, and it is grand.

Sadly, the Straight Guy usually does not consider a repeat engagement, although he will almost always assent to one before getting off the phone. Your only hope with this specimen is to convince him early on of your total compliance with his contact restrictions. Even then, don't count on anything. Just be grateful for your . . . stroke of good fortune, and be prepared to move on. Lightning does indeed strike twice, but rarely in the same spot, and never is it the same bolt.

THE FREAK

Hang on for this one. Then hang up. The Freak is the gentleman who failed to relate in the IM portion of your intercourse that he has a particular fetish. Like the sender of fake pictures, he figures all he needs to do is get you there.

There's no need to list the various and nasty permutations on eroticism the Freak enjoys. Suffice it to say that there are men out there who think a fit of severe, hacking coughing is as sexy as it gets. If such a man cons you into a phone call, cut your losses, save your voice, and get out.

THE CHANGE OF HEART

This is the guy who hangs up on you midwhatever, usually moments into the conversation. This can be rough on the fragile ego. It can also be utterly baffling. The talk begins, it seems to be quickly achieving a desired momentum, and then buyer's remorse suddenly takes your partner. Something in your tone, or something you said or didn't say, has shown him that you will not do after all, and you are summarily disposed of.

Take this with not even a second's worth of dismay. The caller who so abruptly cuts you off because he isn't getting the precise quality of hotness from you that he insists upon is a caller who's looking for a little too much from a make-believe world. He is the phone version of the man who shows up at your door and decides that, your accurate picture notwithstanding, you are not good enough. When, in fact, he's just not playing fair.

THE SHAM

The Sham is the fellow who presents himself to you online in a specific way, as a certain kind of man or boy, and who lives up to this image not one bit when the voice contact is actually made. Sometimes his IMs depict a sweet, passive younger man, and the tone and voice bespeak—quite literally—an aggressive senior citizen; more often, he portrays himself online as a man's man, a real girl-loving jock, and then he sounds a little too much like one of those girls he supposedly chases.

As with an in-person date arranged with the guy who thinks he can put one over on you and take glorious advantage of your heightened state of desire, you owe this character nothing. It may be, as in those actual dates, that the Sham truly believes he is the man he told you he was. Luckily, you don't even have to worry about triggering a dangerous episode here. No, you don't want to hurt anyone if you can avoid it. But—hang up. This is merely phone sex we're talking about, after all. No one's life is at stake.

LIGHTS, WEBCAM, ACTION

ENTER THE WEBCAM.

You may initially believe that this miracle of modern technology requires as much in the way of cameras, tripods, coaxial cable and lighting arrays as a Hollywood shoot. But the webcam, which plugs into your computer, is simplicity itself, and relatively cheap, too. The camera itself, either a sleek penlike gadget or an old-fashioned little robotlike ball, clamps to your monitor or sits by its side. All that's left is the software, and that can be downloaded in a jiffy.

You're ready to go. All you need to do now is find a cam-friendly chat or site, message the exhibitionist dude of your dreams, poise your lens to take in all you want him to see, and drop your trousers. This is virtual sex as literal as it can get—until the holographic, three-dimensional version arrives.

So, are you enjoying it? You haven't even got a webcam? Let's talk about why.

It doesn't matter that vast distance separates you from your new erect online friend. It doesn't matter that he doesn't know who you really are, and that you'll most likely never actually meet. Revealing yourself on the webcam is a big, big step. It goes beyond dirty messaging, beyond pic trading, and beyond phone sex. It is all about *showing yourself*, and showing yourself at your most heightened state of arousal. Which is also, not coincidentally, your most vulnerable. Moreover, in these waters, you can't fake it. This, guys, is not for everyone.

It may seem that the most pertinent factor here, the most obvious explanation for the disinclination of most of us to go webcam, is what we have to offer. If we're not buff, or if what takes up space between our legs isn't taking up all that much space, it's reasonable to assume that we don't want it broadcast on satellite.

Yet that's not all of it. Not—sorry, but it's too there to resist—by a long shot. Because a great many men with nothing to hide and a lot to flaunt just aren't interested in the procedure.

Fast sex is digestable to many of us. We're not gleeful about the sleaze factor intrinsic to the practice, but we acknowledge that we are human, that we have sexual needs and that it's one way of accommodating them. We do it and we chalk it up to adapting, to taking care of business in today's frenzied world. And we keep it to ourselves; these usually aren't the kinds of cyber-generated encounters that make for pleasant conversation at the watercooler at the office the next day.

But except for the most uninhibited, the most lusty, the men most free from societal and cultural constraints, we have limits. Not so much as to what turns us on, but more along the lines of how we can satisfy our desires without sacrificing too much of our sense of selfhood. And a camera capturing us is, more often than not, just too far to go.

Fred broke up with his boyfriend just recently, and not for the first time. The breakup on this occasion, however, was triggered by Fred's discovering that the love of his life had been playing around on webcam sites. Fred felt betrayed, cheated on, even outraged. And his partner was dumbfounded by this reaction. "It's nothing but *porn*, really," he pleaded. Fred countered, "But you're letting someone else turn you on. Someone *real*." The boyfriend paused, then said, "Hey, those Brazilian boys you get such a kick out of in the Kristen Bjorn DVDs are real too. They're just not looking at you while you're looking at them. So what's the big deal?"

The big deal, as the boyfriend above did not see, is that porn stars are not real to most of us because they exist as fantasy beings. The guy with the webcam is much closer to home. No matter how purely sexual the episode was, the two men were *seeing* each other for the purpose of intimacy. In a partner's eyes, there exists the chance that someone on the webcam could fall in love. And in a world where even turning to mass-produced porn can disrupt a relationship, this can be a risky affair indeed.

The day will come—it may come next week, in fact—when newer, slicker technology will make connecting by today's webcam as laughably old-fashioned as the carrier pigeon. Let's go even more madly utopian and say that, when this brighter future dawns, we're all of us going to be as toned and sleekly sexy as the hottest guys in films. I'd still bet that for every individually designed and perfectly executed program allowing sexual intensity to pass between men physically distanced from each other, there will be legions of guys who want nothing to do with the whole business. It's no secret that men often fantasize about being porn stars. But it's equally acknowledged that, by and large, we really don't want to get too near to living out our fantasies. Besides, all those porn stars are never really looking at us. Thank God.

Phone sex. The webcam. Both are essentially nothing more than playthings, occasionally erotically satisfying substitutes for actually getting together with that fantastic guy you stumbled onto online. Which is ultimately what the heftiest percentage of men going into chat rooms are after. Conveniently, the pursuit has name: the hookup.

THE HOOKUP: LET'S BE REAL—PROSTITUTES CALL THEM "DATES" TOO

Baby, I ain't Mr. Right
But if you're looking for fastlove . . .
—"Fastlove," George Michael

IT'S TIME TO ACKNOWLEDGE AND GO INTO THE STRATEGIES of genuine connection. Because sooner or later you will be engineering actual encounters. You will accomplish this through chat room interaction or through the more direct websites devoted to sex between men. Maybe you will place an ad; maybe you will respond to one. However it happens, you will be enjoying physical passion with a real live man. (Well, let's *hope* you'll be enjoying it.)

It's tempting to say here that this is what it's all about. I'm almost *expected* to say here that this is what it's all about. Porn, chats, downloaded videos, phone calls, cam-to-cam connections—these are just playthings, after all. They are the tech stuff of erotic dreams, the toys with which to take care of business when the genuine article is unavailable. We use them, we buy them, we download them, and we delete them. But we'd trade it all—to paraphrase The Doobie Brothers in an insidious way—for just one minute of real sex. Right? Right.

Actually, wrong. Very wrong.

Gay online activity may very well forge a path to gay offline connections. *But it doesn't have to and it isn't always supposed to.* In point of fact, one of the most commendable elements of the whole online scene is that the fantasy it so abundantly provides spares the gay man a lot of scrambling in the real world. Unless he's absolutely driven to be with another man and very soon, he can usually find that the universe of romantic and sexual scenes, and people dancing across his screen is enough—for tonight, at least.

When you sit down at your computer in a lascivious state of mind, you are, at that moment, ready to grab the keys and dash off to where anyone hot is waiting. Then you fool around a bit online, and the urgency to race out of the house wanes. Yes, sometimes the impulse passes because you attended to affairs with no direct assistance. But not always. Sometimes— and this is a truly marvelous feature, or even failsafe, of online doings—the desire simply passes. As desire often does in the real world.

Have you never passed an exceptionally studly man on the street and been so taken you actually began following him, or at least considered a few moments of harmless stalking? Sure you have. But nothing happens, and not just because nothing was ever very likely to under those circumstance. Nothing happens because the tide of your lust ebbs. Nothing happens because reality overtakes fantasy—on the street or at your computer—and desire goes back into its cage.

Desire is not always the mindless beast it is painted as. It is a beast, to be sure. But it has mind enough to know that it can wait. You will be giving it free rein soon enough. There will come times when you want nothing less than a real connection, you want it soon, and you are determined to use every program and application on your computer to arrange one.

REALITY CHECK

Fine. But understand, and understand fully: This is not about love. Straightforward, down-to-business hookups are not recommended for those seeking romance. Don't go into the hookup hoping that it may lead to more than sex. It *may*. It happens. But it must never, never, never be approached with that end in view, because you will most likely come away sorely disappointed.

Why not? Maybe the two of you went into this for fast sex, but the sex was sensational. He seemed like a great guy. And he seemed to think you were a great guy. If the stars were so aligned that you both ignited upon contact, that you emphatically shared an identical passion, why isn't it reasonable to conclude that more will follow?

Because *you did not go there for more*, and neither did he.

It is vital that you recall what this was supposed to be about before you are tempted to call the hookup by another name or develop it into something more. You must remember—and those who do not use their highlighters here are in deep trouble—it is extremely likely that what made the encounter so successful was the very absence of other expectations. It was sensational, not because it was the beginning of something great, but because there was the freedom to enjoy the moment with no dread of consequence. And to anticipate a relationship based on *that* foundation is worse than buying a wedding ring because his eyes are sky blue.

Again, yes, something substantial can emerge from a hookup. Yet this must never be consciously sought at the outset. Do this, and you may as well expect the cute boy who sold you the computer at BestBuy to phone. He had a job to do, you had a reason for being there, and that, as they say, was that.

Now let's talk about caution. If the subject at hand is negotiating sex with men who are virtually strangers to you, you need to understand something about how the gay online cruiser ought to protect himself from the threat of assault or worse.

First and foremost, I sing my favorite song again: Trust your instincts. If anything at all—*anything*—is ringing that bell, *cancel.* Second, teach your desire to hang back just a little. Set up a public meeting first. And there's a valuable clue within this strategy, too: the man who absolutely refuses to consider five minutes over a cup of coffee at a place just down the street is probably trouble.

Then learn as much as you possibly can about the prospective date before even agreeing to meet up with him. Get the facts. Of course, since this isn't a job interview or the first in a series of romantic dates, you're limited as to just how much information you can cull from your friend. And expecting to get substantial vitals in this situation is a little like thinking you can squeeze the melons in an Internet supermarket. This is about steamy sex, and neither one of you is about to waste much time in providing an extensive résumé.

But there are clues given all the time, in even the most smoldering online exchange. The man who's in town on business, for instance; he doesn't have to tell you what his *job* is, but you should find that he's lodging at a local inn, and, if he's genuine, he'll be pressing for you to do the traveling to him. Or maybe he's visiting family on a break from college. If there aren't quite a few limits on his availability in that instance, something's not right. The college boy on break always, always has a full dance card.

Also, no matter what the scenario, let a third party know where you are going and/or something about the guy you are hooking up with. Someone should be aware of the specifics of the encounter, in case something goes awry. There is the unsettling and not wholly satisfactory suggestion in this that the lunatic who hacked you into suitcase-size pieces will be caught. Which is missing something, as safeguards go.

Nonetheless. It makes sense. There are crazy people out there. And to set up a clandestine meeting with a stranger flies in the face of everything we were ever taught as children. So, yes. As soon as the arrangements are made, as soon as you log off and race to gargle before you meet that amazing man, call your best buddy and tell him that someone named VizitnJoc212 is on his way. Or leave a note before you make a dash to the local motel, detailing the room number and what you think you know about your . . . date.

You should do these things. You should make a call, leave a note, and bring a cell phone. Unfortunately, all these measures are still pretty feeble. If the guy you are to meet is indeed dangerous, you are, at least for the time being, on your own. That we are all men here helps a little; the factor of the weaker female threatened by the more physically powerful male doesn't come into play, and the sick bastard who intends harm knows this too. The disturbed prey on the weak. Gay bashers most certainly do. Present yourself as strong—which you will most likely do anyway, for the sake of the sex—and risk is further minimized.

Once more, you should most definitely obey your gut if it's telling you that something's not kosher at any point along the hookup trail. It doesn't matter that whatever's troubling you can't be pinpointed. It doesn't matter that your hookup has thus far not messaged or said anything specifically suspect. That's why it's called "instinct"; it relies on information your conscious mind does not discern. This may come to you upon hanging up the phone, upon turning the key in your door on the way out, upon taking the exit to the Red Roof Inn. Whenever it comes, obey it. If it doesn't *feel* safe, it isn't safe. And far better to turn around, go home, and download a video than to get beaten up.

Did I scare you? Good. Thus do I hyperstress that most valuable, if mysterious, of human talents: one's instincts. *Obey them.*

Now, let's talk about the mistake that dooms the hookup to die at the door.

There is one reason for it: you or him. One of you went out a tad too far on the limb of the tree of lust. One of you allowed desire to tint reality. Or, to throw yet one more metaphor into the mix, one or both of you chose to ignore the red flags and went flying into the arena like a drunken matador. It happens all the time. If it hasn't happened to you yet, it will.

Then, too, there's still the less sensational—but just as date killing—factor of no sparks at all. Call it "failure to launch," call it a lack of chemistry, call it anything at all; it simply translates to a complete absence of excitement of desire when finally meeting up.

When Robert finally got to the appointed room at the local motel, he was unsure if Mark would, in fact, be there. Robert had done everything right, of course. He had sent and received pictures, he had negotiated a relatively lengthy IM conversation—not easy, when both men were feeling intensely erotic—and he had even secured the "public" scrutiny. That is, it was understood that when Robert got to the door, they'd step out for a coffee or drink in the motel restaurant.

Mark answered, and Mark looked just as great as Robert had supposed he would. Robert, too, was the ideal, three-dimensional version of the pictures he'd transmitted. Everything was suddenly looking fine for a well-planned, perfectly conducted hookup.

Except that Robert was back in his car only a few minutes later. Both men *had* done everything quite well. And Robert was eager to get down to business. But Mark wasn't, and for no other reason than that, once in Robert's presence, he was simply not attracted to him. The chemistry wasn't there, period, and Mark was disinclined to fake it. Leaving Robert to go home and accept the fact that just as sparks can ignite when completely unexpected, so too can the right combination of elements utterly fail to catch fire. And it's no one's fault.

The moral to the story of Robert and Mark is that no matter how careful you are, mistakes will happen and/or the passion you anticipated will be lacking. Remember the first admonition, the "no expectations" clause, in this section. And honor it.

Unfortunately, when you yourself are the rejected one, all the calm reasoning in the world won't take the sting away. Being turned down, for whatever reason, isn't a whole lot of fun. However, two things can be learned from these unfortunate occurrences.

First off, you learn that it is always best to be the host. It may seem otherwise; after all, why should it always be *your* towels? But one's turf is one's turf. It is infinitely better to be on your own ground, if you might be wounded. Rejection is disagreeable. It is worse when extended, when drawn out to the car and the road back home. Inside, turned down within your own living room, you can speedily pop in a movie and pretend nothing bad happened. As you didn't have to shell out for gas with a smack to the face as your reward, all the better.

Do not—do *not*—endeavor to place the rejection in a too open-minded and understanding light, one that victimizes you as having fallen short of the mark. Do not think, *Gee, I wish he had liked me because he was really, really hot.* Do not think, *God, what's wrong with me?*

Think, *Okay, to each his own. I was honest about myself, he had no business expecting something else, and the spark just wasn't there.* This is the only sane rationale to adopt, because, if you've been playing the game fairly, it's the whole "why" of the mistake. Cyber communication can transmit much, but—so far, anyway—it can't replace the chemistry required to make for a hot time.

Whatever you do following an aborted hookup, just don't call the guy and leave a bitchy message.

But that's quite enough of warnings. Let's go the zero hour, when it's going to happen. You have gone from chat to chat. You have answered e-mails and given out more stats than an audited CEO. You have messaged and exchanged pictures, you have winnowed the wheat from the chaff, and—hosanna!— you have what we'll call a date. Due at your door in a matter of minutes, or expecting you at his.

Don't panic. Panic is counterproductive. Relax, take a breath, and heed well what you read here. I know what I'm talking about. I have answered a few doors in my time. I have slammed a few shut, too.

- Always *try* to arrange a safe place to meet up with your new friend first. Have him join you for an espresso at a hip coffeehouse before you even consider inviting him to your place or trotting off to his. This is a routine you need to establish as habit if you choose to play in this arena.

All right, lust is impatient. All right, there will be times when you are just too crazed to go this route, and this advice then reads like a mom yelling after her kid to put his galoshes on after he's out the door and knee-deep in the snow. It still has to be said, and it still should be practiced as much as you possibly can.

• Do not transmit your address through a message box to someone you don't know. Do not transmit your address through an e-mail to someone you don't know. If the man you want to hook up with is insisting that you do so—and unwilling, for whatever reason he may put forth, to make a simple phone call to a guy he shortly plans on being very intimate with—you need to find someone else. Someone with a phone. Because the voice you hear on that phone will reveal a *lot*, and will pretty dependably guide your instinct in the direction it needs to go.

• Before you log off and race to the bathroom to gargle, before *anything*, make sure an understanding exists between you and your incipient guest. Think of it as the "no expectations" clause: If either of you doesn't do much for the other one, you shake hands and part amicably. Phrase this however you like but *get it into that final IM or phone call*. For one thing, it's the only civilized way to go, as this failsafe openly takes into account the possibility that you yourself will be perceived as the dud. For another, it's an ego shield for the date. It implies merely that the chemistry might be off. It in no way suggests that his presentation of himself is or was less than fully honest. As many of the visitors you greet through this means will be outright frauds, your chivalry will be unimpeachable. Most important, it's the most expeditious way to get them sliding back out the way they came. (Note: There is an inherent "it's not you, it's me" element of manure within this, yes. But no one has yet devised a better parachute.)

- Don't dress up. In fact, dress down. This isn't a meeting of the Ladies' Fine Arts League.

- Beware the sensational, hot, built guy who is eager to hook up with you anytime you please, and from your first IM exchange, too. The hard reality is that, if it appears too good to be true, it most likely is. Amazing men, generally speaking, either have alternate possibilities always open to them, a warranted level of caution in meeting up with new guys, or both. They never push, and *definitely* never push from the word go.

- Is your expected guest a sexy guy? Would he be expected if he were otherwise? No. So do two sets of push-ups, timed to inflate your pecs minutes before he'll be knocking at your door. If you have dumbbells nearby, do a few fast arm curls, too. The bonus here is that, if the chemistry isn't right and the date lasts half a minute, you will have done something good for yourself in the process.

- As the host—so to speak—it is your duty to soften the shock of the actual first sighting of each other. Make no mistake, it will be a shock. If he has falsified his pictures, it is up to you to instantaneously formulate the polite but firm heave-ho. And if your guest is just as hot as his picture led you to believe, the jolt actually increases in voltage, albeit pleasurably. Even then, however, keep your cool. In this mating game, you stay strong when you don't go weak in the knees. Your own attractiveness is enhanced when his doesn't make you buckle.

- Hide your wallet. No one's telling you to be paranoid. But does it hurt anyone to have his wallet hidden?

- Like any good host, take your cues from the guest when he arrives. For example:

> He enters. He is perfectly hot. But he is awkward, unsure, just standing there. It is up to you to touch him in a way not fully erotic, and not merely buddy-buddy. Clap a hand on his shoulder, but let it remain there for a second or two. Similarly, place your hand for a moment on the back of his arm. If you do it right and convey this welcoming, he will make the next move easier.

> If the awkwardness persists, then persist with the hospitality. Your job is to make this guy feel comfortable. Offer a drink, offer a seat. The more at ease and unhurried you are, the less pressure he will feel. And this will result in the very good time you asked him over for to begin with.

❯ He enters. He is hot and he is *fast*. If you didn't know better, you would have sworn he began unzipping in the damn elevator. In these situations you must not lose sight of the fact that, his ardor notwithstanding, this is your turf. Subtly back away from the hall; he will follow. Keep backing away until you reach the designated romping space. Passion is fine but that won't be *his* Xbox smashing onto the hardwood floor, will it?

❯ He enters. He is laid-back. Enjoy this and go with it, for here you have the erotic opportunity of duplicating the suspense of a bar meeting with the thrill of knowing the outcome to it. Offer a drink, by all means. Sit a spell. The tension thus generated won't last long, believe me, but it will add immeasurably to whatever follows.

• Towels, towels, towels. Be sure to have a few readily accessible. You're the host, remember. Carved guest soaps in the shape of tiny shells are another matter, and don't apply here.

• Passion is a thirsty business. Have some cold water or juice on hand to offer.

• If he was hot, you were hot, and the whole episode was hot, excellent. But don't destroy all your good work in the farewell. This is crucial. Too often the host of the encounter plays his cards perfectly, then shatters the machismo of the episode with a too-eager plea that it be repeated, and soon. Again, take your cue from the guest. He will not be shy in affirming that he has indeed had a swell time. Then and only then, once his enthusiasm is safely on record, can you ease *his* mind and concur. And, as a good host, mention how another get-together would please you enormously. Repeat performances do happen, after all.

But if it's not in the cards, don't take it as a reflection on yourself. There are many reasons why men won't revisit even the most satisfying hookup scene: guilt, fear of starting a relationship, the hookup's thrill lying in the singleness of the occasion, or merely the fact that there is still a world of hookups yet to explore.

• Sometimes—for it is an unfathomable world—your partner leaves silently, even sullenly. You don't get it; everything seemed to go swimmingly, and you were sure that he was glad to have visited. But he skulks out with barely a word. And you chalk it up to a lapse in your ability to gauge another person's state of mind.

Then, often later that very night, he e-mails or phones. He thanks you. He even asks when you're free again.

Don't beat yourself up or second-guess when he exits mysteriously. There is, again, a multitude of reasons why he might have been uncomfortable and eager to get out when the fun was done, and most are identical to the reasons guys don't pursue a second encounter after a great first one.

Often it's a case of his simply just not knowing how to exit decently; this isn't, after all, a social experience with rules and standards learned in school.

Answer the e-mail, take the call. And forget the unimportant slip in his manners.

STOOD UP BY THE HOOKUP: DEALING WITH THE MAN WHO GOT AWAY

THERE ARE BUMPS AND BRUISES HAPPENING ALL THE TIME, as real life intertwines with online life. We try to inject a little of real life into online life all the time. We want the people we deal with online to practice the same degree of basic consideration they do offline. Just as we try to.

Yet the fact remains: Online intercourse is, to most people, less than real. We are all wizards when connected to the Internet; we can make anyone disappear with a click, and we ourselves can disappear from anywhere in the land of cyber interaction with a speed and dexterity to dwarf Harry Potter's graduating class. The reason why is our business, if we're harried and wanting out. Added to which, power corrupts.

So despite all of your best efforts to conduct yourself online as you do three-dimensionally, the escape hatches are just too many and too accessible. They will be used. If not by you, then by a fellow chatter who got a bad case of buyer's remorse after agreeing to hook up.

If this hasn't happened to you yet, it will. It may even happen when you would have bet the farm that your date was etched in stone. Your partner was salivating, was in town, was dressed and on his way out the door. Your partner may even have called from his car, needing further directions or wanting to underline the urgency of his lust. Then he didn't show.

What this situation requires from you is an altered sensibility, and nothing more. Yes, it is annoying and frustrating to be left standing at the altar of passion under any circumstances. And it's a boot to the ego to be stood up, whether by someone you actually met, or by the fabulous man you know only as MuscJockGA. But never forget in what terrain the connection was generated. Your encounter took shape on a plane where fantasy is king. In such a place, shifts of landscape happen like lightning, mood changes with the change of the song playing in the background, and no one is real if the other someone doesn't want them to be real.

There's something else, too, and it's not pretty. Just as certain dudes flex and strut like mad in chat rooms to generate the adulation they require, some purposefully and vigorously set in motion meetings they have *no intention* of attending. They will IM you; they will present fantastic images of themselves; they will avow that your pictures are driving them crazy with desire; and they will tell you that getting together with you—as soon as possible—sounds like just the ticket. You're where? A few miles away? Well, then— let's do it.

Then, when you ask for something like a number to call, they will not respond. Or it will be a while before they reply, and the reply will unaccountably refer back to what was already well established. Or they will suddenly invent a tissue-thin roadblock, something so nonsensical you can dispel it in a flash. No matter how they slip away, they slip away because that was the only thing they ever actually meant to do. Beyond getting off on getting you all hot and bothered, that is.

All you can do when one of these supreme teasers strikes is jump ship when the first excuse comes, or when the response is especially delayed and hedges all over the place when it does finally appear. You may have been had, but not for long.

Sadly, such men have been out there for a long, long time. Ask any woman. These guys were practicing a specific form of fantasy gratification long before there was an Internet. Gay online communication merely gives them a richer field in which to play.

Once upon a time, a guy named Mike spent hours trying to get a very interested, very hot guy named Bill to come to his place. The pics had been traded, the desires established; the only obstacle seemed to be that Bill was inexplicably reluctant to make the short trip to Mike's door. Mike *should* have seen the all-too-clear sign, but he wasn't thinking all that lucidly at the time. He just kept asking. Finally, finally, Bill agreed. Mike e-mailed him directions to his house—never a smart move—and he waited on the porch for him to arrive.

Bill never arrived. Someone else did. A someone else, it turned out, who had also been in lengthy communication with Bill. In other words, Mike and his visitor were both duped by the same player.

But a wonderful little turnaround was the result. You see, the visitor was understandably embarrassed. He, after all, was the dupe who actually did the legwork in Bill's scam. Mike saw his embarrassment, and found that it made this cute young guy even cuter. So Mike asked him in. Then, with the forged bond of having been victimized by the same jerk, something ignited, and the two had a very fine time.

It gets better. Bill messaged Mike that evening, checking on how his devious manipulation had panned out and probably looking forward to seeing Mike rant and rave on his screen. What Mike did was thank him. What Bill did was sign off, pissed.

OTHER ISSUES,
OTHER ANSWERS

A LOOK AT THE ONLINE
BISEXUAL MAN

TO A HETEROSEXUAL PERSON, IT MAY SEEM ODD TO DEVOTE
an entire book to the subject of men pursuing sex with other
men online. Trust me, everything here is only scratching the
surface.

There is another, quite pertinent, raison d'être for this
book. The online explosion itself, as was stressed earlier, is in
fact responsible for substantially altering one hitherto tidily
tucked-away element of real life. American males who have
long been accustomed to exercising any latent fantasies about
being with other men only within the confines of what their
minds can conjure, now have access to all the gay guys who
want them and all the other guys like themselves who had no
safe, easy outlet in which to explore these desires.

In other words, this guide is for *men* online. It is primarily
directed to the gay man, but there are so many other men out
there in gay chats, men who adamantly refuse to be identified
as "gay," that I'm not entirely sanguine in even saying that
this guide is for gay, bisexual, and curious men. Even such a

wider categorizing has to be dispensed with because it is still too limiting. There are just too many men out there who are, or who claim to be, curious. There comes a point when we must stop handing out name tags and wave the whole damn crew in.

Remember, gayness and homosexuality are no longer one and the same, if ever they were. You may snicker at the "straight" guy who occasionally engages in sex with another man, yet who perceives himself to be defiantly heterosexual. But don't be so quick to laugh. The world has yet to legitimize the crucial distinction that what we think of as "gay" is a way of living that encompasses behavior, viewpoint, societal interaction, political affiliation, etc., while a sexual act may *indeed* be nothing but a sexual act. And when it comes to men, a sexual act is usually very little else. Ask any woman.

Still, though, why *are* so many men who are ordinarily decent, ball-playing, child-producing, Budweiser-drinking men seen in chat rooms where female charms play no part at all? The answer lies not within gay dreams of straitjacketed straights, but in the very basics. The answer is in the sheer sexuality of the male beast.

Someone made a handsome buck claiming that men are from Mars. Men are not from Mars. Men are from the woods. Not to put too fine a point on it, males like to ejaculate a lot, and are spared the female's encoded need to latch on to the partner so that the issue produced will be provided for. It's really that simple.

All right, then. But don't most men just want women? Sure. But most goats very likely prefer fresh vegetation to tin cans, yet will feast on either. And if tin cans were forbidden fruit in goatdom, you can bet those beasts would be sniffing around the General Foods warehouse whenever opportunity allowed and other goats couldn't find them there.

Also, it won't do to ignore the monolith of male vanity. For reasons that honestly elude me, it is evidently rather a hot tribute to the straight man's ego that another man is pleasuring him. This creates in the adventurous straight dude the notion that he is a free thinker. You yourself probably know more than a few macho dudes who boast of "exploring their bisexuality."

Booze, ego, a girlfriend too long out of town. Whatever the reason, multitudes of men are glad to have some form of sex with another man at some stage of the game. Men practicing bisexuality is big business these days. The Internet genuinely has opened a huge door in society, and it's a back door. The man who once toyed with the idea of homosexual fun now has more validation than he could have dreamed of, because now he has seen that thousands of other men—real men just like himself—are interested too. Moreover, the entire scene is exponential in growth; each man discovering, and then participating in, the online game of hunt and capture with other men frees at least several of his neighbors to do precisely the same thing. And so on, and so on.

When women bemoaned the advent of ESPN, they didn't know what real trouble was.

PORN SITES, DATING SITES, AND YOUR CREDIT CARD

Dig if u will the picture
—"When Doves Cry," Prince

IN AN ALTOGETHER REAL SENSE, ALL THAT'S BEEN THUS far discussed is pornography. Make no mistake, the sexually oriented chat room is nothing but a variation on it. Men who actually do generate encounters from chat room meetings are out there, to be sure, and their numbers are legion. But an even greater multitude jump into the rooms for the vicarious thrill of exchanging filthy dialogue and nude photographs with other people.

It's strange. After all, the models who pose and perform on the porn sites are people too, aren't they? So why the bigger kick from the everyday mold?

The answer to that is temporally based. Smut must always be new to be optimally exciting. The soldier boy on that nasty site you like, the one who fell on his back and pretended to resist the onslaught of the faux staff sergeant, fell a while back. Even if the footage and/or pictures were taken only days before, it is old news. But when the soldier boy with whom you are at that moment messaging describes in vivid detail how the carpet feels on his spine, you are there. You are once again in the realm of method acting. It is better to be in the moment.

Don't be concerned, though, for the old-fashioned porno sites. They are in no danger of going away, certainly not from lack of visitors. Name the fetish and it has a multitude of web pages devoted to it. To even begin to tap into the most minimal listing of them is, as well you know, a bridge way, way too far. Hairy guys, Asian guys. Male genitalia—gargantuan or petite. Seas of rear ends like acres of apple orchards. Latex, spandex, sneakers, and circus clowns. There is no need to list, and no likelihood of listing with any degree of conclusiveness. It is probably a good thing—in an amoral sense—that just about every taste or prurient inclination out there has so many enthusiasts that a wide selection of prosperous sites cater to it. If the bedrock to successful capitalism is that nice little formula of supply and demand, online pornography is the truest yardstick of its validity. Sites go up and come down every day, thousands of them, and only the smart ones survive. It is American commerce at breakneck speed, a billion billboards jockeying for position on the superhighway of the Internet age.

The upscale dating venues want your business just as eagerly. There's a virtual universe of porn and romance sites out to get your hard-earned buck. So let's draw your attention to a few seemingly obvious, but too often ignored, elements of these vendors. It's merchandise, after all. No matter what part of you it's meant to appeal to, some clear reasoning is called for.

• First and foremost—the pay porn sites. The best thing to tell you would be to have nothing to do with them. There is no need to pay; there are zillions of pages and sites that will accommodate your needs nicely and not cost you a penny. This is absolutely true.

But you're going to join a few anyway. We all do, mentally relegating the monthly tab into little more than the price of a latte we just might stop for every other day on the way to work. Then, it is naive to expect that a free page will be quite as up to date, as laden with unseen images and videos, as those pages that exist to entice you into extracting your credit card anyway. (Note: It probably indicates something disturbing that the same strategy of "only pennies a day!" is used both to entice people to finance meals and shoes for orphan children overseas, and to download raw footage of young men on spring break.)

So here's the rule: *If you have to pay for it, it better be better than real life.*

• Here's the second rule, and disobey it at your future's peril: *No more than two monthly charges at a time. If you can afford it.* Do not scoff at the grandmotherliness quality of the admonition. In a state of intense arousal and focused like a demon at your screen, you may as well be drunk off your ass. Your judgment is elsewhere. In these hours it is painfully easy, in about three seconds, to rationalize yourself into someone who would normally chug five lattes on the way to work. Every day. And who is now channeling those funds in a different and far more urgent direction than sating caffeine addiction.

- Third rule: *Thoroughly check out what the site offers before you type in your credit card info.* Most porn sites offer various memberships. There's the famous three-day pass for a few bucks, the great enticer of those of us horny but still not without a sense of fiscal responsibility. Unfortunately, many such cheap deals limit the content available to you. Movies, as a rule, get viewed only by those signing up for a monthly hitch.

  Given the predominant restrictions, and given the general price range of monthly fees gay sites charge, we suggest you take the plunge—if you must—and go for one full month. You will pay between $19.95 and $29.95, the higher prices customarily getting you lots more straight men going mad.

- But whichever site you choose to make your provider for that month, mark well all the fine print at the bottom of the entry page. This will tell you—and they try desperately hard not to—how to cancel before you are automatically rebilled for the next month. Curb your lust for the short time it takes to bookmark this information, or write it on the handy pad beside your desk. You will be astonished at how, ten minutes after joining, buyer's remorse will strike as overpoweringly as your libido so recently did.

- "No charge for a trial membership" indeed. Rather than rant at these spurious cyber pickpockets, though, remember what you must already know: if you type your credit card information onto any single porno website's screen, your credit card is going to be charged if there is any way on earth they can do so. There is no gorgeously sophisticated program within these lusty places that will patiently wait until your three-day introductory phase is done and then politely tap at your bank's window. Nor will any one of them subtract the ballyhooed mere $2.95 it suckered you in with, then leave you to go on your merry way. They are there to carve a hefty $29.95 or $39.95 out of your Visa, and they will gleefully do so unless you dot every *i* and cross every *t* regarding your options to have nothing more to do with them.

REALITY CHECK

All the above notwithstanding, here's some sound advice: pay for nothing and wait until you can't wait any longer. Then even those pictures online since before the flood will take on fresh and thrilling life. The supreme advantage to this strategy—aside from all the latte you can actually now purchase—is that you will feel positively Machiavellian about your business acumen when the . . . chore is done. You will be relieved of tension *and* not burdened with the nagging sense of having dropped more money for something you would, right then, swear you had no use for anyway.

- It's far easier to be extravagant with your wallet when you're shopping for your dating/personals site. This isn't porn; this is real-life stuff, and the site that can get you together with the man or men of your dreams feels more like an investment and less like a seedy indulgence.

Okay. That's a good argument. Just type out and print the following little list, and tape it to your computer monitor.

1. Many of the men in my locale with ads on one site have ads running—for free, typically—on the other major gay dating sites too. I will remember this before I even think about subscribing to or paying for multiple sites.

2. Just as these men patrol all the waters of the various sites, I can too. Free.

3. The site I'm signing up for and giving money to is the site that best reflects my own inclinations. As a gym jock/leather man/skinhead, Jockbod.com/Leatherweb.com/Worldskins.com is the right site for me to subscribe to.

4. So far, my investment in this particular dating site is/isn't paying off. I'm keeping track of when I joined and what my success ratio is. It's fine/lousy, and I think I'll stick with it/cancel and move on.

• Take full advantage of the many male-specific porn directories out there. These obliging folders delineate thousands of pages and sites, and update them constantly. Hunkhunters.com is an awfully well-designed example of such, as is Manpics2000.com. Most of what they link to is free, they update by the minute, and thousands upon thousands of sites are offered up. If you aren't getting the very best in digital porn and still-wet images, the vastness of the selection more than compensates. And there is often gold to be found in these mountains, too.

• Do some homework. In the past year alone, certain gay weblogs began offering free downloadable up-to-date porn, and more of them are doing it every day. What usually occurs is that you click on a picture of the video you want, and you are immediately taken to a file-sharing space. These sites—what site doesn't?—would like you to subscribe. They promise that once your fee is banked, you won't have to wait a minute or so to get your download going, as the nonpaying user must. As with all offers, the choice is yours. Just remember that even in the most frenetically sexed-up state you find yourself in, a minute is not a very long time to wait.

• If you are tossed like a canoe in an ocean storm onto a page you never sought, and the content of the page is at first unclear to you, get the hell out of there. Mysterious links are everywhere, especially on porn sites. You already know how many fetishes are broadcast online. Torture is among them. Even uglier sides of humanity are explored too. Click. Click hard, click fast. Make it disappear. Otherwise, you run the very real risk of lingering a moment too long and seeing what no human being should ever see.

• The gay porn passes include, but are hardly limited to, Global Male Pass (GMPass.com), ManCheck.com, and United Gay Adult Sites (UGAS.com). (The latter is a personal favorite, if only due to that solidarity-driven name.) These passes exist to protect the victimized porn purveyor from horny little minors. That, anyway, is what it's all supposed to be about; the credit card number is the badge of the adult, so the usage of it secures the porn website from bad and illegally young would-be attendees. What is interesting, though, is that the webmaster may pay the pass people, and so do we. Or the pass people may pay the webmasters and then shake us down. However it's done, you are reminded of *The Godfather*. Yet the gay pass is not, all things considered, a bad deal. It can be the smartest use of your porn dollar.

But shop carefully. Before you subscribe for a year or two, examine the listings of sites each pass provides access to. There is a sort of general slant to each, a bias that sets them apart from the rest. Again, take the time to do your homework. Note which sites tend to employ which pass, and you'll see a pattern develop. You might choose to subscribe to one because of a single very hot site's dependence upon it. This is not especially extravagant. As some of these sites update regularly and creatively, thirty bucks for two years' worth of access ain't bad.

Nevertheless, you have to wonder how long even the most generous of these middlemen can survive. With each passing day, gay porn blogs offer for free what these merchants of only a year or two ago were looking to collect upon. It actually appears that porn, gay or otherwise, is becoming so widespread that the currency is changing. With hundreds of gay porn blogs now happily linking surfers to free video, porn itself is being rendered as inalienable a right as walking down the street.

• The "lifetime" pass is an option that now exists at most of these sites, and at a pretty decent price, too. It makes you wonder just how successful this marketing ploy is. The deal is good, without a doubt. But mortality isn't something most of us like to work into the equation when weighing which pages have better naked men on display. It's easier on the psyche to think that after a certain age is reached, you're going to leave it alone.

• Hacked pass sites (the notable gay ones number approximately a dozen or so) are based on the most delightful manure you'll ever stumble upon in the fields of online life. That is, they *purport* to exist to alert the abused, hacked, expensive gay porn site to the passwords for his emporium that are currently being bandied about illegally and unpaid for. That, on paper, is their sole reason for being. It is beautiful. Not since Mr. Haney wheeled his cart of garbage into the Douglas' yard on *Green Acres* has there been such bold chicanery.

Of course the hack sites exist to lure the devilish peruser into reaching for his credit card, either to actually purchase a membership to one of the sites broken into, or—more commonly—to pay the hacker itself to break into sites for him all the time.

Yet this is all a little too much like a deal with Satan. Granted all the waters you wade in hereabouts are murky. But signing up to pay for a partner in online flimflam? Steer clear. It isn't likely you'll have your knees broken by thugs in the employ of webmasters. But you nonetheless want to avoid messing around in such a bad part of town.

STAYING CONNECTED

IT WILL HAPPEN. IT HAS, IN FACT, HAPPENED TO YOU. IT IS almost enough to make you trash your machine and return to the primitive world of cruising on the streets, as our forebears did.

An ideal IM chat is occurring on your screen, and you are half of it. You had no idea this sort of specimen existed in your town, and it is doubly miraculous that he is intently pursuing you. You click to transmit maybe the most vital message—what time, your phone number, etc.—and the hourglass of your pointer remains an hourglass. For a while. For forever. Then— if you're an AOLer—that voice, that far too eager real estate salesman voice, calls out from your speakers: "Good-bye!"

Nerves on fire, you go to red alert. You bite the bullet and kill the power. And then you chew your nails as you wait out the interminable minutes it takes for your computer to reboot and for you to get back online. Eventually you are back. He is gone. He has been snapped up like a reduced-to-nothing designer blazer on a rack in T. J. Maxx.

I've been online through various ISPs. No fly-by-nighters, each is a respected and powerful provider, a major player in the rich market of the monthly billing of millions of users. Each one stays with me as a provider of something else, too: ISP help never given. The longer you are acquainted with your machine, the less, thank God, you need help. You begin to understand the nature of the beast; what you can't fix just then, you learn, isn't really broken to begin with, but just stalled.

But it still happens that glitches stick around too long to remain glitches, and become serious barricades to your online time. You need help, and your tech-smart pal isn't answering his cell. So you look for the number of your ISP's technical assistance department. They finally pick up. And far more often than not, you waste hours obeying instructions and engaging in pointless activities that don't begin to address just why you can't stay online.

So, first and foremost, when things are going awry: *Do not call tech support.* Do not toy with the idea of calling tech support. If you live next door to tech support and your house is burning down, do not call tech support. The reasons:

• See "modem string" in the tech terms glossary. I am not kidding.

• Nine or ten years after having been assured that defragmenting your drive would make your ISP connection stick—as, back in the nineties, so many of us were instructed—you'll still be ashamed and angry at having swallowed this fable.

• There is something less than reassuring about an assistance network that asks if you are online when they are there to help because you cannot get online. It makes you mistrustful. How much faith would you invest in the Coast Guard if their standard response to an SOS was advising to start the motor and point the boat to shore?

• Those new and many fix-it options available from every ISP out there? Not good. Your computer will react to these like a child with his head held back in a parental vise, being dosed with cod liver oil. He may ingest it, after struggling. But odds are, he will not retain it and your nice clean shirt will be covered in spittle. In other words, don't go there. These downloads will, nine times out of ten, get you nothing but a series of fresh pop-up ads.

• It's fairly a given that the tech support people polishing their fingernails and advising you to rewrite your modem string have seen every possible filthy screen name imaginable. They are probably sworn to confidentiality agreements, and sign lots of nondisclosure sorts of papers. I don't care. It is still unacceptable to be engaged in a nondirty phone conversation with someone who knows that you are, at least part of the time, BonedUpnNeednIt.

The hard fact is that the tech support offered by AOL, AT&T Worldnet, PeoplePC, NetZero, EarthLink, and all the other big boys is today's equivalent of the elementary school nurse. The best you can hope for is a place to lie down and shut your eyes for a few minutes.

What can you do, then, to insure a stable link to all those men out there waiting to drive you crazy in a good way? Let's look at the three options.

DIAL-UP. This connection, sharing time with your landline and violently subject to the flows of Internet and telephonic traffic, is still not a bad thing for the very occasional Internet user, or the guy living so deep in the Midwest that a run to the grocery store means saddling up a mule team. For the rest of us—fuhgeddaboudit. It is simply, painfully, excruciatingly *too slow*.

DSL, OR DIGITAL SUBSCRIBER LINE. This second bowl of porridge is almost just right. Almost. As it depends on a phone line reserved solely for your Internet link, you enjoy much faster action with page-loading, file downloads, and such. On a good day, in fact, you'd swear you had a cable hookup.

The downsides? You are still suckling, as it were, on your phone company's teat. This translates to a dependence on a system that is pretty damn antiquated to begin with. And the quality of your connection relies on the telephone wiring within your residence. For most of you, that's not a problem. If, however, your home is older and the phone wiring archaic, you may be in for some very jerky online sessions. Or you may be thrown offline every time it rains heavily and water gets into the basement.

Wireless service is an extension of the DSL—or cable—experience. It basically translates to installing a gadget that transmits the Internet connection from one computer to another in the same household, allowing both to share the hookup. It works. A lot of the time.

But with DSL it will *only* work as well as that initial connection is going. And you must share the single link's bandwidth with whoever is busy at the other computer. You'll be surprised, too, by just what a tangle of cords and wires are required to set up a "wireless" link.

Ultimately, DSL isn't a bad way to go. But it's still a Ford to the sleek Mercedes of . . .

CABLE. With a cable hookup, before you sit down you are at the website you want to go to. It isn't that it is *fast*; it is simply that you are connected to all of it, every minute. There is no loading time. There is only the going there. As of this writing, there is no better Internet hookup.

Just beware: Before you order the cable, or even the DSL, understand that being online virtually 24/7 means that you are vulnerable to every pop-up infestation, virus, spam, and all the other bacteria of cyber life out there. If you're not skilled in setting up appropriate safeguards, find a friend who is.

Also, cable is not cheap. Calculate just how much of your time is occupied online. Obviously, if your business—even from home—or your primary shopping, your mail, your researching, your blogging, your whatever, relies on the Internet and is a hefty chunk of your life, go for it. Investigate the packages increasingly offered from cable providers that for one fee give you Internet access *and* approximately 3,500 television channels to peruse.

Factor into your decision the intensity of your online cruising and the time spent doing it. If you are a relatively normal gay male, you will be writing the check to your local cable provider before I finish typing this sentence.

TECH TERMS
AND CHAT SLANG

The following list of basic computer terminology is woefully abridged. The definitions themselves are poor, glib, or poor *and* glib. Yet I swear to you, I have been online since 1993, and what you see below has served me and my needs amply, and well.

Also, very little here relates to the pursuit of sexual gratification. But a mild dose of dry fact never hurts.

AOL *(n)* America Online. The most popular ISP, still. The most full-of-itself ISP. The most expensive ISP. Like IBM, it has *power*, and big friends. AOL is to ISPs what the megamall is to shopping destinations; it's a little too frantic, a little too gleeful, a little too out to please. And it is far, far too damn colorful. It has in fact been forced to drastically alter its marketing strategies in the face of fresher providers. A subscription to AOL will still cost you a solid twenty-four bucks a month, but availing yourself of their e-mail is absolutely free, whether you belong or not. As of this writing—and as of my own termination of my relationship with them—further uncharged-for inducements are on the horizon.

The web is opening up in a big way, and AOL is scrambling to keep the fortress together. . . . But many millions still use it, its inability to actually provide the connection itself notwithstanding, because many millions of us are very used to it. Moreover, the AOL marketing strategy of leaving its start-up disks on every surface in every American public place—like a maniacal weight trainer planting rice cakes in his overweight client's path—is just too hard to bypass. (Note: America Online, way back when, desperately wanted to be known as AO. It didn't take. Possibly because the acronym makes the speaker sound like a Harry Belafonte impersonator.)

AOL SUCKS *or* **SUX** *(slang)* The battle cry of the chat room whiner. This particular phrase exploded into the heavens back in 1996, when AOL first offered unlimited usage for a set price and, astoundingly, did not foresee that this package would trigger a surge of usage big enough to make that comet that killed the dinosaurs look like a pebble tossed by a toddler. Echoes of the phrase are heard today, as AOL's determination to add Pink dancing on your welcome screen unfailingly short-circuits the basic functions you signed on for.

APPLICATION *(n)* Something the driver may or may not do. It doesn't matter; once you're forced to deal with application problems, you need real, geek help.

CRASH *(v)* When your hard drive is too stressed to go on. The mouse pointer freezes on the screen, nothing clicks, and you must reboot and pray that the hot soul mate you were IMing with will understand, or not turn to another soul mate before you can get back online.

DEFRAG *(v)* "Defragmenting," the maid of your computer. It shuffles all those stray little files back where they belong, and permits you to believe that the embarrassing stuff you deleted from your hard drive is now truly powder. When, in fact, a savvy FBI agent can dig it all out in a jiff.

DESKTOP *(n)* The screen you look at before you go online. The desktop is the pagan altar of modern times; utterly unimportant, people spend hours festooning theirs with icons and pictures that reflect what they're all about, and that practically no one save themselves will ever see.

DISKETTE *(n)* Those 3.5" things that can store—with, they tell me, still only relative safety—your vital documents, valuable letters, and images of porn stars' asses. Today's personal computer, however, not only allows you to burn your material onto a CD, it doesn't even deign to have a place in which to stick a diskette, rendering diskettes pretty much as outmoded, as receptacles of information go, as stone tablets.

DRIVER *(n)* No one knows, but whatever it is, it doesn't actually *move*.

EMOTICON *(n)* Those variously expressive circles of face you can plug into e-mail, messages, whatever. They are clearly loved, as AOL introduces hundreds more—some with sunglasses!—with each yearly upgrade. They are what, if your child persisted in drawing them, you would emphatically not magnetize to the refrigerator door. (Note: I make no attempt to dissemble my dislike of emoticons. I am not especially spiritual, but I suspect that when it rains in hell, emoticons are the rain.)

GIGABYTE *(n, pl)* Much more memory than the wee megabyte, but doomed to the scrap pile soon, as new games, movies, and such require great heaping gobs of them. Not long ago the sleekest machine you could buy boasted four gigs of memory. Today the meal equivalent to four gigs is a spritz of Cheez Whiz on a Ritz.

FILE *(n)* Anything that goes into a folder.

FOLDER *(n)* A file with other files in it.

HARD DRIVE *(n, kick-ass variety)* The intestines of your computer.

ICON *(n)* A big star, so big that he or she is representative of an era or genre. That's in real life. On a computer screen, it's a tiny cartoon of something.

ISP *(n)* Internet service provider. AOL is an ISP. NetZero, EarthLink, MindSpring, and PeoplePC are other ISPs, but how much fun can they be? They charge less, and therefore can't afford to illegally ship in immigrant tech support on the scale of AOL.

MEGABYTE *(n)* An amount of memory, but not a lot. Sort of like a forgetful aunt.

MODEM STRING *(pain-in-the-ass n)* What tech support at AOL makes you rewrite when you can't get online and they have no idea what's wrong. It looks like an equation for a radioactive weapon stolen by the Soviet enemy, when there was a Soviet enemy: a chorus line of capital letters and numerals, and even some esoteric punctuation marks for good measure. It is actually of supreme unimportance. The modem string is the cod liver oil of online life.

OFFLINE *(adj, adv)* Not connected to the Internet, and sane.

ONLINE *(adj, adv)* Connected to the Internet, and horny.

PC *(n)* Personal computer, aka babysitter, best friend, worst enemy, dirty bookstore, neighborhood tavern, door to the world, and irritating window blind to the world that keeps snapping shut.

PHISHING *(v)* A homonym for "fishing," this word refers to the practice of sending out phoney (foney?) e-mails in order to get the recipient's banking information. As you probably know all too well by now, "phishing" is both big business and increasingly sophisticated in its mechanics. Fortunately, the online arms race comes to the rescue. For instance, for every neatly executed fake eBay e-mail conning the user into signing on—and thus transmitting his password to the "phisher"—an eBay alarm is sounded and the accounts are locked down.

But the best safeguard of all is that even if you absolutely believe that eBay or Bank of America or Seancody.com sent you that e-mail, *never access the site in question from the link within the e-mail.* Go to it through a bookmark or old-fashioned URL, and you will be unharmed.

RAM *(n)* Random access memory. Apparently this is the queen on the chessboard of your hard drive, and lets you run many things to and from many places. Beyond that, you're on your own.

REGISTRY *(n)* Simply, the configuration database in the Windows world. The registry holds the settings for the hardware and software of the PC, and under the scary names of SYSTEM.DAT, USER.DAT, etc. More simply, if you begin to get messages that your registry is experiencing problems, you will be shopping for a new machine in the near future.

ROM *(n)* Read-only memory. Doesn't do nearly as much as RAM, but you need it.

SCREENSAVER *(n)* Screens were originally sensitive beasts, and burned out their irises when left too long inactive. Thus the screensaver was born. That the modern monitor is protected from burnout has done nothing to stem the tide of screensaver options still out there. These are provided by your machine in the form of desert flowers, strikingly ugly geometric patterns, and something that looks like an Italian cottage wall with a window from a very space-age hospital built into it. Or you can create your own, using dirty pictures. Go to Appearances in your control panel. After you gather up and save the dirty pictures.

SOFTWARE *(n)* All the games, programs, smut, alien invasions, crosswords, etc. you can upload, download, send, and fiddle with.

SPAM *(n)* The e-mails you get from Donna!, who saw you in a chat room!, and has a friend who sells Viagra!

VIRUS *(ghost n)* Mostly mythical, this creature roams the cyber world, scaring millions and compelling millions more to buy antivirus programs perpetually outdated by new viruses.

Note: PC user, listen up. For every drive threatened or crashed by a virus, thousands more are hopelessly screwed up by the unnecessary and costly implementation of protection devices. The reality is that too many people have rendered their own machines damn near useless by trying to safeguard them. Those who have been disabled by a virus are relatively few, hopefully because few people are imbecilic enough to download a graphic in an e-mail from someone named Doomsday. The virus is the hurricane striking the trailer park; those whom it gets are those who see it coming on the Weather Channel but just won't budge from their double-wide.

WINDOWS *(n, in the sense that God is a noun)* The Spielbergian-in-its-genius concept behind the online explosion. Give the people boxes of pictures instead of text, call them "windows," and Bill Gates can buy Europe.

CHAT SLANG

The abbreviations of parts of speech are omitted. Recall that this is the realm of messaged, made-up talk. Assigning grammatical function here is somewhat like playing tag in a tank of full of eels.

A&F Also "AnF," or "Aber." Refers to the Abercrombie & Fitch brand of clothing, a dependably sturdy and generally plain line favored by jocks, buff college dudes, and the like. The young man who incorporates these initials in his screen name is an ambitious soul indeed, as he seeks to marry the concept of being a tough straight guy with the screamingly gay fetish for broadcasting an admired designer. It makes you wonder how Banana Republic missed out on this pervasive and subliminal means of getting the word out; its name so much more readily lends itself to the chat room user's love of obvious double entendre.

ASL "Age, Sex, Location." This triple-threat census demand is often slammed into chat rooms, ostensibly so that the really busy cruiser can weed out the old, honest geezers in Willow Falls, Montana, that much faster. It may seem odd to the new user that the *gender* of the occupants in an M4M room forms part of the inquiry. It will seem less odd once you have examined a few profiles.

AVERAGE Used most commonly in reference to body type. In real life, it means "average." Through the carnival mirror of online doings, it means fat and/or flabby.

BAREBACK Engaging in intercourse without employing a condom. Unfortunately, the snazzy, yippee-kai-o-kai-ay, daredevil feel to the word falls just a little short of the recklessness it refers to; by this standard of description, arson may be defined as browning marshmallows.

BEAR Referring to a physical type appealing to quite a few men, the bear is sometimes muscular, sometimes portly, usually middle aged and always, always hairy. It implies a high degree of masculine behavior. At least, it does to the novice. In reality, the average bear is docile of manner and often submissive in sex.

BEER CAN A tin receptacle for malt beverages. Here, the accepted metaphor for the all-around dimensions of a chatter whose little fireman boasts more than respectable girth.

BI "Bisexual." As put forth by a man, it means he enjoys sex with women or men. As put forth by a man online, it means that he kissed a girl once, back in high school. Or almost did.

BOTTOM The name of the agreeable ass in Shakespeare's *A Midsummer Night's Dream*. Online, it's a preference, if not insistence, on being passive during intercourse. In other words, an agreeable ass.

BRB "Be right back." As messaged in an IM, it is a catchall breather. It can refer to anything from the user's genuine need to take a call or visit the john, to his strategy of hoping you just go away. It is in essence a slightly more narrowly interpreted aloha.

BTW Quite possibly the most stupid acronym in the entire history of trendy wordplay. Short for "by the way," it saves the busy, busy person exactly five letters to type.

BUFF Short for "buffed," to indicate an athletically toned physique. Here you learn, as elsewhere in life, that pecs are more in the eye of the beholder, and not necessarily actually on the beholded. See **HUNG**.

C "Cut," or "circumcised." The have-not of the online male, and a surprisingly definitive line in the sand for many an online cruiser. See **UC**.

CATCHER See **BOTTOM**.

CD "Cross-dresser." A man who enjoys wearing women's clothing. The most well-known reverse instance of this practice—women suiting up as men—resulted in the billion-dollar *Annie Hall* craze of the seventies.

CHAT ROOM In a sense, the chat room is the reality of the cyber interactive experience. It is nothing. That is, it actually exists only through user activity, as it can only be defined by the particular activity going on within it. So it can be anything, from purgatory online to a frenzied and exciting space bursting with hot men, from a Greyhound station with no one but you and a homeless guy sleeping on two chairs to the club where you first encountered the best date you ever had.

And when it appears that you're facing endless bus depots, you can create your own room too. That's the great thing about nothing; we all own it.

CURIOUS How a man refers to himself when he wants to come across as heterosexual but interested in gay encounters. What it more realistically translates to is much oral sex with other men and a deep need to be anally violated.

CYA No, not an acronym. It is a slang good-bye, the hipster's "See ya," as in "See you later." It's like the children's book about the bee, *C D B!*, wherein the pronunciation of the letters tells the story of the industrious insect: C D B? D B S A B Z B. . . .

DISCREET Often abbreviated in a variety of forms, "discreet" points to a Boy Scout level of trustworthiness regarding keeping your little online and offline hobbies secret. "Discreet" means your wife, girlfriend, or boss will never know if we wrestle around a bit. "Discreet" also has the distinction of being perhaps the most commonly misspelled word in all of online usage. After, of course, the impossibly complex and diabolical duo of "to" and "too."

FACE This is the thing on the front of your head. As written in an IM, it is a demand that you show what you really look like above the neck via a transmitted photo. Increasingly a sine qua non in the hunt for transient partners.

GF "Girlfriend." The Loch Ness Monster of M4M life. There may be no hard evidence at all of her existence, yet we believe. This is the creature referred to by the guy who really wants you to believe he's straight, or by the guy who wants even more to believe it himself.

HANGING OUT What absolutely everyone is doing online, when asked what they are doing. Essentially, nothing at all. Also phrased as "just hanging out," "hangin'," or—and this comes from the straightest of the online boys—"kickin' back."

HOOK UP Scarily accurate, this phrase for meeting for a sexual encounter. For built within it is the hope or plan that one of you will be swinging off of the other.

HOT Three little letters that, strung together, mean . . . everything. Hot is good-looking, built, hung, sexy, cute, handsome, killer, studly, adorable, and any single one of these or any combination thereof. "Hot" is what turns you on. "Hot" is also how someone "hot" makes us feel, and "hot" is the typical assessment of whatever activity we then enter into, either in reality or cybernetically. If you're IMing and you think he's hot, he thinks you're hot, and one of you has in mind something hot he'd like to be doing with the other, then the whole thing is—that's right—*hot*.

HUNG In the real world, the term by which a male informs the world of his member's superior size. Online, it means that he has one. A member, not size.

IC "I see." Here is where the witchcraft of language comes into play. An IM correspondent will reply with this pithy pairing of letters after you affirm that, yes, your roommate is gone and you can indeed hook up at five. Yet no matter how enthusiastically he pushed for this very hookup, his "IC" reads as . . . well, icy. Often followed up by a "BRB."

IM Instant message, the modern way to annoy from the comfort of your home. AOL advertisement example: "Hey, Joey! Coach here. You're pitching today!" Real online example: "Hey, dude. Coach here. Bend over."

LOL "Laughing out loud." This is typed in rooms and in IMs by people who want other people to know that they are audibly laughing. Men scratching outlines of woolly mammoths on cave walls had more sophistication. But in all fairness, the Internet is a very shorthand kind of world.

LOOKIN "Looking?" Often sent as a freestanding IM sans question mark. This interrogatory is the text version of the hand dropping to the crotch area paired with the smoldering gaze. Somebody likes your profile, you killer, you.

LTR "Long-term relationship." This is what all those people searching the rooms for fast sex are currently and happily in, or this is what all those desperate to hook up within the hour for even faster sex are searching for with all their heart.

MASC "Masculine." That would seem pretty clear-cut, would it not? It not. In fact, "masc" has been more debased by lack of substance than the pre–World War II deutsche mark. Sadly, it is so overused that if you don't automatically add "masc" to your self-description these days, you may as well be in your third trimester.

MFM "Male-female-male," the jovial marker of the honest-to-God semistraight fellow, which indicates his desire to include a lady or two in the party. (Note: As in those strange locales that can't be arrived at in the same way in which they're left, the eager *respondent* to such an identifier is usually tolerant of a woman within the scene only as the gal who mops up the room when it's over. That is, the guy usually after the MFM man wants him bad, but wants absolutely nothing to do with the women who turn that man on. But, boy, does MFM get those hands shooting up at the desks.)

M4M "Men for men." A surprisingly cryptic code, as many a young dude will enter TRUCKERSM4M and demand to know where all the gurlz R.

MM "Married man." Often "MWM," or "married white man." A grain of salt·may not be sufficient seasoning with which to take these labels, for too often are they employed as basic protection devices for the male who wants sex and does not want a date. All in all, however, they are harmless lies. And in this sphere, it's better to flirt with someone who likes barricades.

PBP *or* **PARTNERED BUT PLAY** This designation says a lot. It's used by the guy who is in a relationship of one kind or another, but a relationship with an understanding: extracurricular sex is allowed. So the PBP man is good for a good time, but hands off when it comes to more serious intent.

PIGPLAY Okeydokey. "Pigplay" is everything funky. The man into it is into spit, scat, water sports, bondage, spanking, verbal abuse, physical abuse, or any combination of the above. The word is general but the intent is always sleazy, messy, and nasty. If "pigplay" is a sort of gay sex buffet—and it is—it's a buffet laid out in the garage. And not for the faint of heart or dainty of appetite.

PNP *or* **PARTY AND PLAY** This little tag indicates something of a wild man, because the "party" is meant to point to a liking for recreational substances. And the "play" usually means that group sex is high on his list.

PRINCE ALBERT *or* **PA** This is a male organ pierced with a ring usually—and presumably reduntantly—connecting the shaft and what we'll call the helmet. There's a lesson here for all of us who once thought nose studs the depth of jewelry excess.

ROFLMAO "Rolling on floor, laughing my ass off." WIGWFBWTSC? (What is God waiting for, before wiping the slate clean?)

S2R "Send to receive," i.e., if you want to see me naked, you send a picture first. If I think yours is real, I'll return one of mine. If I doubt the veracity of yours, I won't send mine. If I know yours is a fake but is hot anyway, I may oblige. Etc., etc.

SCAT When I was young, this meant singing meaningless syllables to a jazz riff. It still does. In an M4M profile, it indicates a lust for feces. And to think, I used to frown upon meaningless jazz syllables.

SHRIMPING Not a liking for cruising little people, as we once naively thought, "shrimping" involves making love to your partner's toes. How you go about it is entirely up to you.

SIXPACK *or* **6PACK** *or* **8PACK** These numerical lust triggers refer to the abdominal wall muscles and are customarily boasted about by users who will flee the country before accepting a message from someone over twenty-five years of age. "Sixpack" has replaced "swimmer's build" as the code for alluringly slender, and serves as well as the keystone to the arrogant strut of the online boy.

STATS "Statistics." Age (roughly), height, weight, dimensions of torso, arms, waistline, and whatever inch mark is selected when you close your eyes and stick a pin near the far end of a ruler.

STR8 "Straight." This would appear to mean "heterosexual." Not online, it doesn't. In a man's profile, it means that most anything goes, except kissing.

SUP "Wassup," in itself a bastardization of "What's up?" It's still a fairly commonly employed hello, all right. But it seems to be moving to the slang garbage heap, to be thrown on top of "dude." And only the very young dare use it, ever.

SURFING As in "surfing the Internet." This attractive phrase refers to the activity of clicking on link after link and going from site to site, with no objective at all. In real life, this is called being a bum.

SWIMMER'S BUILD Purely defined, this means lean and sleekly sexy. In online life, this translates to someone equipped with only the muscles required to type; scrawny, yet often with a chunky waist. Interestingly, this description has pretty much faded out of cruising terminology, so false has been its history. (See **SIXPACK**.)

TEABAGGING A practice involving the dropping of the testicles into the partner's mouth, perhaps to the beat of the old Lipton jingle. "Brisk, brisk, brisk! . . ."

TEA ROOM Apparently, gay culture can't get enough of Ye Olde British Empire: Prince Albert, teabagging, and now this. A "tea room" is a bathroom, and you'll see these words pop up on many a chat dialogue screen.

TOP He who does the doing, in anal intercourse. Also known as "pitcher," for those who can't fathom sexual practices outside of a baseball context.

TS "Transsexual." Take a guess. Yes, that's right. The TS—or almost always the one in gay chats, at least—is the man who has undergone or is undergoing procedures to change his gender.

TWINK By no means strictly an online creation, "Twink" is nonetheless a much-used item in the cyber vernacular. Short for "Twinkie," this truncated expression for the snack cake refers to a boyish type: slender, usually hairless, and young. It implies as well a persona; the Twink is generally passive, compliant, and sweet of nature. (Think Leonardo DiCaprio. It doesn't matter that age-wise he has gone well beyond Twink status. Leonardo DiCaprio is so of the mold that he will die a Twink.)

UC "Uncut," or "uncircumcised." And if you think this a relatively unimportant specification, you are too new to online gay cruising or you are straight. Either way, glad to know you.

UR "You are," or "you're." I rather wish the sexier hillbilly slang of "yer" fit this bill. But I don't make the rules.

VERS "Versatile," in a sexual top-or-bottom way. We see this more and more, as increasing numbers of gay men embrace the hitherto untapped markets available through multitasking.

VGL "Very good-looking." An acronym hauled out primarily by those who spend hour after happy hour within the cushiony walls of subjective realities. As with its granddaddy acronym "VIP," the label appeals more to seekers than to genuine possessors. Yes, some self-tagged VGL users are at least GL. Some are even V. But most who choose to slap this gold ribbon upon their buff chests belong under the banner of an even more ancient acronym: OK. (See **HUNG.**)

WS "Water sports." Another extremist preference, WS refers to sex involving urine.

WITCH To "witch" is to lead a guy on, either in cyberspace or in the flesh, and then fail to deliver. (No, this isn't the most widely employed gay slang for this phenomenon you'll come across. But I was really, really determined to end with something other than "WS.")

THE BEST ONLINE GAY RESOURCES

BEFORE ANYTHING AT ALL IS LISTED HERE, YOU NEED TO keep in mind what you already know very, very well: Internet life is a fickle thing. Sites go up and sites come down every minute, and a few of the best disappear as frequently as a lot of the worst.

But some sites . . . well, they're not going anywhere soon. These are the dating and porn sites already mentioned; they take their place with the recommendations below, shoulder to shoulder with other real survivors.

FOR GAY NEWS

Your best bet here is 365gay.com. A compendium, 365gay culls the latest—and I mean the latest—in gay issues of national and global interest from media outlets everywhere, and lists it all neatly for you. Gaywired.com, the Gay.com news page, Bgay.com, etc., are on the same track. But 365gay covers all the territory, and faster than anyone else.

There's no getting around it. The little book of bars that Bob Damron first published in 1964 paved the way for the most comprehensive selection of online gay travel options you could ask for. Damron.com may be relied upon fully.

That said, also explore gay-oriented travel through *nongay* means. Take, as it were, an indirect route—search for where and how you want to go using the hundreds of superlative travel sites available, from Priceline.com to Travelocity.com, and *then* seek out the gay-friendly options at your destination. You may want to stay in a gay B&B in Maine. But that doesn't necessarily mean you need to ride up there in the gay car on the gay train.

FOR SHEER FUN

Bettybowers.com. This is hands down the cleverest, most bitchiest, most marvelously fun location a gay man can find online. Not recommended, however, for the truly religion-sensitive man.

FOR HOOKING UP

As of this writing—and the sincere endorsements of the dating sites spoken of in the "Sites" chapter notwithstanding—Manhunt.net seems to be the most effective and increasingly most turned-to site out there today for hooking up. Others are larger, and many others have been around for longer, too.

But Manhunt.net ain't slowing down. And its own momentum seems to fuel the men posting on it. No other similarly sizable gay site in my experience is more focused for men who are looking to meet up for dating and/or a quickie. Manhunt.net, in fact, is the website that came to the rescue in the story told in the prologue. I bring it all home now, because the site continues to grow, and continues to attract the element you're looking to attract.

FOR GRATUITOUS FUN . . .

. . . or, porn.

I suddenly remember the guy—true story—who had just bought a computer and who asked me how to find pictures of sex on the Internet. Plug the machine in, I said.

It's been mentioned often enough—here, on TV, in the news—that there are a skazillion websites and pages devoted to gay porn online. But a few take the trouble to gather it all up and break it all down for you. So once more I suggest Hunkhunters.com. If it's gay, it turns you on, and it's not somewhere in this site—you're not and never have been remotely interested in men.

FOR WHAT YOUR GAY NEIGHBORS ARE THINKING

There is the blogosphere.

There are hundreds of gay weblogs enjoying great

popularity. Some are intensely and angrily political, others proudly narcissistic and staunchly devoted to nothing but sexy pics and videos. The premier blog in this realm, however, appears to be Towleroad.com. Blogmaster Andy Towle posts snippets of news and gossip, most of it a blend of serious gay issues and lighter, entertainment-oriented stuff. A legion of followers then falls into line to comment, argue, offer counterpoint, and sometimes go for the other guy's throat.

But why not just head straight to the directory? Bestgayblogs.com is it. This place will provide you with links to just about every gay blog out there. Celebrities and gossip, gay rights, gay sports, personal and sometimes beautifully written gay diaries, and the previously mentioned suppliers of free hardcore videos: It's all in here, guys, on one very long blogroll.

Be warned: When you enter the blogosphere, scatter a trail of bread crumbs behind you or you may never find your way home.

AFTERWORD: LOGGING OFF NOW

HAS THIS MODEST VOLUME BEEN HELPFUL AT ALL? I SINCERELY hope so.

I acknowledge that there is much to the realm of the online pursuit of romance, be it serious dating or outright sex, that's been dealt with in this book too fleetingly or not at all. Given the subject matter, I had to conclude that the readership's major defining attribute would not be a lengthy attention span. So I finish with one more look at what surely is the watchword of the whole shebang: "Life's too short." This time, a literal look.

What you do in your own time is your own affair. A lot of us waste a great deal of it, just as we also put much of it to good use. This is the human animal, with or without a box that connects him to all the others. More and more of us have the box, of course. So we're spending more and more time on the Internet. There are, I think, greater sins. And that is the bedrock of the light philosophy of this book.

Go online. Enter chat rooms, strike up a conversation with

that guy you think you'd like to maybe date, engage in dirty talk with like-minded souls, pull up the filthy website when the mood strikes you and the coast is clear. Keep it sensible, keep it to sane levels of time consumption, and keep it as honest and as real as you reasonably can. Treat and view this Internet as exactly what it is: another tool. It can be an instrument for harmless play, and it can open doors to great things. Even at the harmless play level, it's still a valuable piece of equipment.

Basic mindless fun, be it romping through an eighteenth-century cornfield with the farmhands or darting through sexy instant messages, is and always has been a necessary facet of human life. To revile one forum, as the Internet has been so condemned, for catering to that is specious and unfair. There were eighteenth-century farmhands who went too far too. Again, the issue is one of relativity. No arena that man as a social animal enters into is especially harmful when his behavior within it is grounded in sanity, perspective, and humor.

So log on and have a bit of enjoyment. You may well have many grand times at the computer, thinking that life is too short. At those times you are, of course, quite right. Life is too short when life is at its most appealing.

But as we've seen elsewhere, length isn't everything. Thanks, and cya.

Jack Mauro has been a columnist for OutPersonals.com since 2005. His articles on gay romance have also been featured frequently on edgenewyork.com, gaywired.com, 247gay.com, and a host of other men's sites. He lives in his adopted home of Knoxville, Tennessee.